C# Deconstructed

Discover How C# Works on the
.NET Framework

Mohammad Rahman

Apress®

C# Deconstructed

ISBN-13 (pbk): 978-1-4302-6670-9

ISBN-13 (electronic): 978-1-4302-6671-6

Publisher: Heinz Weinheimer
Lead Editor: Ewan Buckingham
Technical Reviewer: Damien Foggon
Editorial Board: Steve Anglin, Mark Beckner, Ewan Buckingham, Gary Cornell, Louise Corrigan, Jim DeWolf, Jonathan Gennick, Robert Hutchinson, Michelle Lowman, James Markham, Matthew Moodie, Jeff Olson, Jeffrey Pepper, Douglas Pundick, Ben Renow-Clarke, Dominic Shakeshaft, Gwenan Spearing, Matt Wade, Steve Weiss
Coordinating Editor: Jill Balzano
Copy Editor: Lisa Vecchione
Compositor: SPi Global
Indexer: SPi Global
Artist: SPi Global
Cover Designer: Anna Ishchenko

To my family.

Contents at a Glance

Contents

About the Author

Mohammad Rahman is a computer programmer. He has been a programmer since 1998 and for the past seven years he has been designing desktop and web-based systems for private and government agencies using C# language in Microsoft.NET. Currently he is working as a computer programmer and earning his doctorate as a part-time student at the University of Canberra, Australia.

About the Technical Reviewer

Damien Foggon is a developer, writer, and technical reviewer in cutting-edge technologies. He has contributed to more than 50 books on .NET, C#, Visual Basic, and ASP.NET. He is the co-founder of the Newcastle-based user group NEBytes (www.nebytes.net). He is also a multiple MCPD in .NET 2.0 onward. Damien can be found online at http://blog.fasm.co.uk.

■ ■ ■

## CHAPTER 1

Introduction to Programming Language

The basic operational design of a computer system is called its architecture. John von Neumann, a pioneer in computer design, is credited with the architecture of most computers in use today. A typical von Neumann system has three major components: the central processing unit (CPU), or microprocessor; physical memory; and input/output (I/O). In von Neumann architecture (VNA) machines, such as the 80x86 family, the CPU is where all the computations of any applications take place. An application is simply a combination of machine instructions and data. To be executed by the CPU, an application needs to reside in physical memory. Typically, the application program is written using a mechanism called programming language. To understand how any given programming language works, it is important to know how it interacts with the operating system (OS), software that manages the underlying hardware and that provides services to the application, as well as how the CPU executes applications. In this chapter, you will learn the basic architecture of the CPU (microcode, instruction set) and how it executes instructions, fetching them from memory. You will then learn how memory works, how the OS manages the CPU and memory, and how the OS offers a layer of abstraction to a programming language. Finally, the sections on language evaluation will give you a high-level overview of how C# and common language runtime (CLR) evolved and the reason they are needed.

Overview of the CPU

The basic function of the CPU is to fetch, decode, and execute instructions held in read-only memory (ROM) or random access memory (RAM), or physical memory. To accomplish this, the CPU must fetch data from an external memory source and transfer them to its own internal memory, each addressable component of which is called a register. The CPU must also be able to distinguish between instructions and operands, the read/write memory locations containing the data to be operated on. These may be byte-addressable locations in ROM, RAM, or the CPU's own registers.

In addition, the CPU performs additional tasks, such as responding to external events for example resets and interrupts, and provides memory management facilities to the OS. Let's consider the fundamental components of a basic CPU. Typically, a CPU must perform the following activities:

- Provide temporary storage for addresses and data
- Perform arithmetic and logic operations
- Control and schedule all operations

Figure 1-1 illustrates a typical CPU architecture.

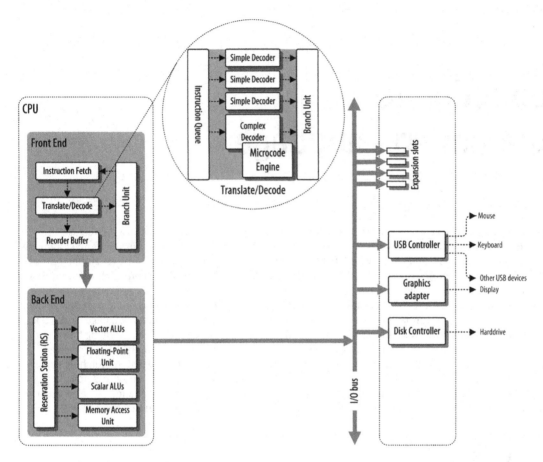

Figure 1-1. *Computer organization and CPU*

Registers have a variety of purposes, such as holding the addresses of instructions and data, storing the result of an operation, signaling the result of a logic operation, and indicating the status of the program or the CPU itself. Some registers may be accessible to programmers, whereas others are reserved for use by the CPU. Registers store binary values (1s and 0s) as electrical voltages, such as 5 volts or less.

Registers consist of several integrated transistors, which are configured as flip-flop circuits, each of which can be switched to a 1 or 0 state. Registers remain in that state until changed by the CPU or until the processor loses power. Each register has a specific name and address. Some are dedicated to specific tasks, but the majority are general purpose. The width of a register depends on the type of CPU (16 bit, 32 bit, 64 bit, and so on).

REGISTERS

- *General purpose registers*: Registers (eight in this category) for storing operands and pointers

  - *EAX*: Accumulator for operands and results data

  - *EBX*: Pointer to data in the data segment (DS)

  - *ECX*: Counter for string and loop operations

  - *EDX*: I/O pointer

  - *ESI*: Pointer to data in the segment pointed to by the DS register; source pointer for string operations

  - *EDI*: Pointer to data (or destination) in the segment pointed to by the ES register; destination pointer for string operations

  - *ESP*: Stack pointer (in the SS segment)

  - *EBP*: Pointer to data on the stack (in the SS segment)

- *Segment registers*: Hold up to six segment selectors.

  - *EFLAGS (program status and control) register*: Reports on the status of the program being executed and allows limited (application-program level) control of the processor

  - *EIP (instruction pointer) register*: Contains a 32-bit pointer to the next instruction to be executed

The segment registers (CS, DS, SS, ES, FS, GS) hold 16-bit segment selectors. A segment selector is a special pointer that identifies a segment in memory. To access a particular segment in memory, the segment selector for that segment must be present in the appropriate segment register. Each of the segment registers is associated with one of three types of storage: code, data, or stack. For example, the CS register contains the segment selector for the *code segment*, where the instructions being executed are stored.

The DS, ES, FS, and GS registers point to four *data segments*. The availability of four data segments permits efficient and secure access to different types of data structures. For instance, four separate data segments may be created—one for the data structures of the current module, another for the data exported from a higher-level module, a third for a dynamically created data structure and a fourth for data shared with another program.

The SS register contains the segment selector for the *stack segment*, where the procedure stack is stored for the program, task, or handler currently being executed. All stack operations use the SS register to find the stack segment. Unlike the CS register, the SS register can be loaded explicitly, which permits application programs to set up multiple stacks and switch among them.

The CPU will use these registers while executing any program, and the OS maintains the state of the registers while executing multiple applications by the CPU.

Instruction Set Architecture of a CPU

The CPU is capable of executing a set of commands known as machine instructions, such as Mov, Push, and Jmp. Each of these instructions accomplishes a small task, and a combination of these instructions constitutes an application program. During the evolution of computer design, *stored-program technique* has brought huge advantages. With this design, the numeric equivalent of a program's machine instructions is stored in the main memory. During the execution of this stored program, the CPU fetches the machine instructions from the main memory one at a time and maintains each fetched instruction's location in the instruction pointer (IP) register. In this way, the next instruction to execute can be fetched when the current instruction finishes its execution.

The control unit (CU) of the CPU is responsible for implementing this functionality. The CU uses the current address from the IP, fetches the instruction's operation code (opcode) from memory, and places it in the instruction-decoding register for execution. After executing the instruction, the CU increments the value of the IP register and fetches the next instruction from memory for execution. This process repeats until the CU reaches the end of the program that is running.

In brief, the CPU follows these steps to execute CPU instruction:

- Fetch the instruction byte from memory

- Update the IP register, to point to the next byte

- Decode the instruction

- Fetch a 16-bit instruction operand from memory, if required

- Update the IP to point beyond the operand, if required

- Compute the address of the operand, if required

- Fetch the operand

- Store the fetched value in the destination register

The goal of the CPU's designer is to assign an appropriate number of bits to the opcode's instruction field and to its operand fields. Choosing more bits for the instruction field lets the opcode encode more instructions, just as choosing more bits for the operand fields lets the opcode specify a greater number of operands (often memory locations or registers). As you saw earlier, the IP fetches the memory contents, such as 55, and 8bec; all these represent an instruction for the CPU to understand and execute.

However, some instructions have only one operand, and others do not have any. Rather than waste the bits associated with these operand fields for instructions that do not have the maximum number of operands, CPU designers often reuse these fields to encode additional opcodes, once again with additional circuitry.

The instruction set used by any application is abstracted from the actual hardware implementation of that machine. This abstraction layer, which sits between the OS and the CPU, is known as instruction set architecture (ISA). The ISA provides a standardized way of exposing the features of a system's hardware. Programs written using the instructions available for an ISA could run on any machine that implemented that ISA. The gray layer in Figure 1-2 represents the ISA.

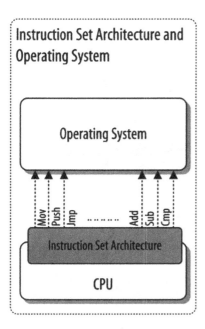

Figure 1-2. *ISA and OS*

The availability of the conceptual abstraction layer the ISA is possible because of a chip called the microcode engine. This chip is like a virtual CPU that presents itself as a CPU within a CPU. To hold the microcode programs, the microcode engine has a small amount of storage, the microcode ROM, which contains an execution unit that executes the programs. The task of each microcode program is to translate a particular instruction into a series of commands that controls the internal parts of the chip.

Any program or process executed by the CPU is simply a set of CPU-understandable instructions stored in the main memory. The CPU executes these instructions by fetching them from the memory until it reaches the end of the program. Therefore, it is crucial to store the program instructions somewhere in the main memory. This underlines the importance of understanding memory, especially how it works and manages. You will learn in depth about memory management in Chapter 4. First, however, you will briefly look at how memory works.

Memory: Where the CPU Stores Temporary Information

The main memory is a temporary storage device that holds both a program and data. Physically, main memory consists of a collection of dynamic random access memory (DRAM) chips. Logically, memory is organized as a linear array of bytes, each with its own unique address starting at 0 (array index).

Figure 1-3 demonstrates the typical physical memory. Each cell of the physical memory has an associated memory address. The CPU is connected to the main memory by an address bus, which passes a physical address via the data bus to the memory controller to read or write the contents of the relevant memory cell. The read/write operation is controlled by the control bus connecting the CPU and physical memory.

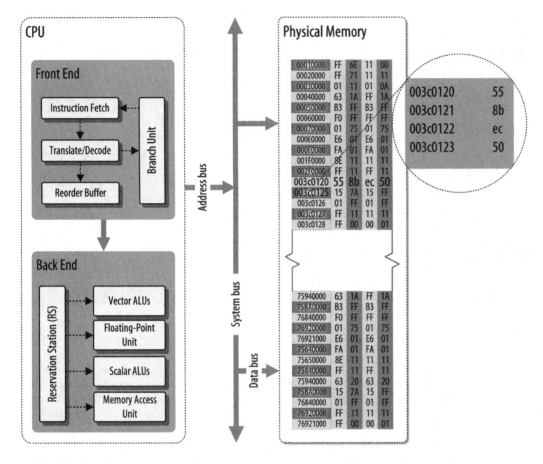

Figure 1-3. *Memory communication*

As a programmer, when you write an application program, you do not need to spend any time managing the CPU and memory, unless your application is designed to do so. This raises the issue of another kind of abstraction, which introduces the concept of the OS. The responsibility of the OS is to manage the underlying hardware and furnish services that allow user applications to consume the hardware and functionality.

Concept of the OS

The use of abstractions is an important concept in computer science. There is a body of software that is responsible for making it easy to run programs, allowing them to share memory, interact with hardware, share the hardware (especially the CPU) among different processes, and so on. This body of software is known as the operating system (OS). The OS is in charge of making sure that the system operates correctly, efficiently, and easily.

A typical OS in fact exports a set of hundreds of system calls, called the application programming interface (API), that are available to applications to consume. The API is intended to do a particular job, and as a consumer of the API, you do not need to know its inner details.

The OS is sometimes referred to as a resource manager. Each of the components of a computer system, such as CPU, memory, and disk, is a resource of that system; it is thus the OS's role to manage these resources, doing so efficiently and fairly.

The secret behind this is to share the CPU's processing capability. Let's say, for example, that a CPU can execute a million instructions per second and that the CPU can be divided among a thousand different programs. Each of the programs can be executed simultaneously during the period of 1 second and can continue its execution by sharing the CPU's processing power. The CPU's time is split into processes P1 to PN, with each process having one or more execution blocks, known as threads. The CPU will execute the processes one by one, but in doing so, it gives the impression that all the processes are executing at the same time. The processes thus result from a combination of the user application program and the OS's management capabilities. Figure 1-4 displays a hypothetical model of CPU instruction execution.

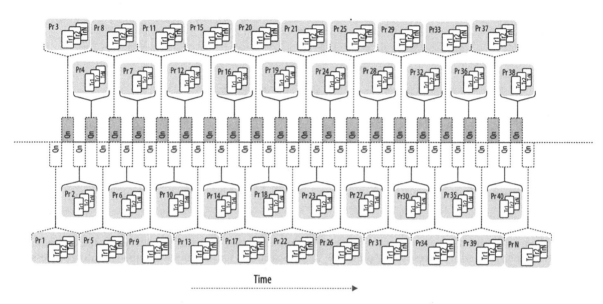

Figure 1-4. Hypothetical model of CPU instruction execution

As you can see, the CPU splits and executes multiple processes within a given period. To achieve this, the OS uses a technique of saving and restoring the execution context called *context switch*. Context switch consists of a piece of low-level code block used by the OS. The context switch code saves the current state of the execution of a process and restores the execution state of the previously stored process when it schedules to execute. The switching between processes is determined by another executive service of the OS, called the *scheduler*. As Figure 1-5 illustrates, when process P1 is ready to resume its execution (as the scheduler schedules process P2 to restore and start its execution), the OS saves the execution state of process P1.

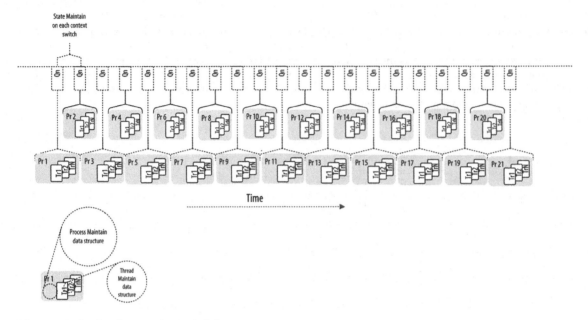

Figure 1-5. *Saving the context to switch between processes*

To save the execution state of the currently running process, the OS will execute low-level assembly code to save the general purpose registers, PC, as well as the kernel stack pointer for that particular process. When the OS resumes previously stopped process, it will restore the previously stored execution state of the soon-to-be-executing process.

Concept of the Process

A process is the abstract concept implemented by the OS to split its work among several functional units. The OS achieves this by allocating a region of memory for each functional unit while executing. These functional units are defined by the processes. Processes contain resources; for example, the CLR has the garbage collector (GC), code manager, and just-in-time (JIT) compiler. In Windows a process has its own private virtual address space (see Chapter 4), which is allocated and managed by the OS. When a process is initialized by Windows, it creates a process environment block (PEB), a data structure that maintains the process.

The OS does not execute processes. A process is a container for functional units; the functional unit of a process is a thread, and it is the thread that is executed by the OS (technically, a thread is a data structure that serves as an execution unit for the functional units defined by the process). A process can have have a single or multiple threads. In the next section, you will explore more about how the thread works in the OS.

Concept of the Thread

A process can never be executed by the OS directly; it uses the thread, which serves as the execution unit for the functional units defined by the process. The thread has its own address space, taken from the private address space allocated for the process. A thread can only belong to a single process and can only use the resources of that process. A thread includes

- An IP that points to the instruction that is currently being executed

- A stack

- A set of register values, defining a part of the state of the processor executing the thread

- A private data region

When a process is created by the OS, it automatically allocates a main, or primary, thread. It is this thread that executes the runtime host, which in turn loads the CLR.

What Is Virtualization?

I have already introduced several abstraction concepts used in computer systems, as indicated in Figure 1-6. On the processor side the ISA offers an abstraction of the actual processor hardware. On the OS side there are three abstractions: files as an abstraction of I/O, virtual memory as an abstraction of program memory, and processes as an abstraction of a running program. These abstractions, provided by the CPU and OS, as well as the API facility of the OS, bring us to the concept of programming language.

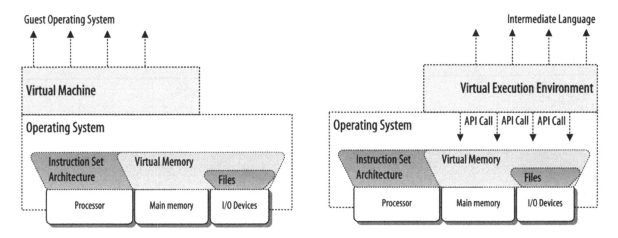

Figure 1-6. *Layers of abstraction*

In layperson's terms, programming language is a mechanism by which you can use your computer's resources to perform various tasks. In the following sections, you will briefly look at the concept of programming language.

Programming Language

You have seen how the CPU's instructions abstracted as the ISA. The ISA helps the programmer write the application program without having to worry about the underlying hardware resources. This abstraction concept introduces a programming language concept known as assembly language. Assembly programming language was introduced to manipulate the CPU's mnemonics programmatically by providing a one-to-one mapping between mnemonics and machine language instructions. The way this mapping has been achieved is by using another piece of software, called the assembler. The assembler is responsible for translating the mnemonics into CPU-understandable machine language. Assembly language is tightly coupled with the relevant hardware.

An application written to target a particular platform requires rewriting when it targets a different platform. The nature of this coupling caused programmers to seek out an improved version of programming language, compared with assembly language. This need ushered in the era of high-level programming language, with the help of a *compiler*. A compiler is software that is more capable and complex than assembler. The main task of a compiler is to transform source code written using high-level language into low-level language, such as assembly or native code.

Compilation and Interpretation

A compiler is a program written using other, high-level language. A compiler is responsible for translating a high-level source program into an equivalent target program, typically in assembly language. A typical compiler performs many tasks, including lexical analysis, preprocessing, parsing, and semantics analysis of the source code. A compiler also generates the target code from the source code and performs the code optimization. Lexical analysis is a process that is used to convert a sequence of characters from the source code into a sequence of tokens. In the code generation phase, the compiler compiles source code into the target language. For instance, when C# source code compiles, it translates the source code into intermediate language (IL) code. Figure 1-7 illustrates the major elements of a compiler program.

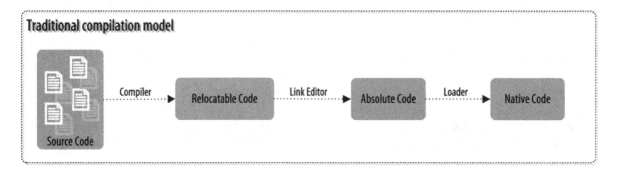

Figure 1-7. Traditional compilation model

Birth of C# Language and JIT Compilation

As you have seen, a compiler compiles the source code into the target language, such as assembly language. There is a one-to-one relationship between the source code and the target code the compiler generates as compiled output. This one-to-one mapping raises the issue of interoperability, which in turn introduces the need for a mechanism that can compile the source code into common intermediate language (CIL) so that later, during the execution time, that intermediate code can be compiled into native code. This gives the flexibility of having multiple high-level languages targeting one intermediate language. Furthermore, that one intermediate language can be compiled into machine-understandable native code. A compiler that acts on this compilation process is known as a just-in-time (JIT) compiler.

One such JIT compiler is that of the CLR. Any .NET language targeting the CLR, such as C#, VB.NET, Managed C++, and F#, will be compiled into the IL. Figure 1-8 demonstrates how C# languages use the JIT compiler at runtime.

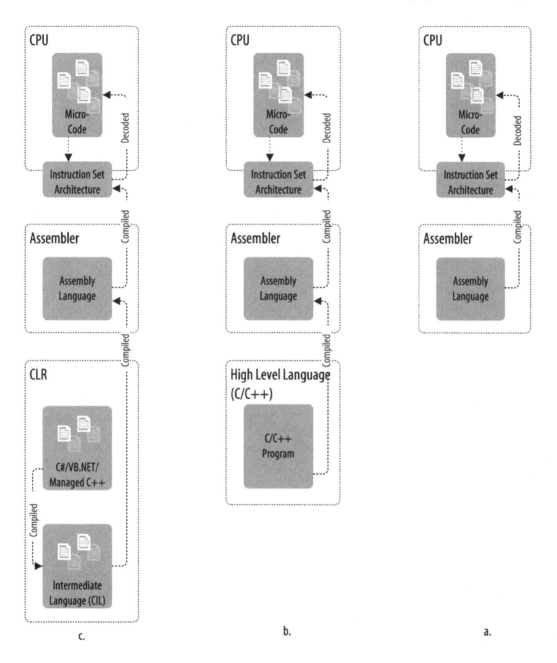

Figure 1-8. *JIT compilation*

Listing 1-1 shows a simple program that calculates the square of a given number and displays the squared number as output.

Listing 1-1.

```csharp
/* importing namespace */
using System;

/* namespace declaration */
namespace Ch_01
{
    /* class declaration*/
    class Program
    {
        /* method declaration */
        static void Main(string[] args)
        {
            PowerGenerator pg = new PowerGenerator();
            pg.ProcessPower();
        } /* end of method declaration */
    }/* end of class declaration */

    public class PowerGenerator
    {
        /* constant declaration */
        const int limit = 3;
        const string
                    original = "Original number",
                    square = "Square number";

        public void ProcessPower()
        {
            /* statement*/
            Console.WriteLine("{0,16}{1,20}", original, square);
            /* iteration statement*/
            for (int i = 0; i <= limit; ++i)
            {
                Console.Write("{0,10}{1,20}\n", i, Math.Pow(i, 2));
            }
        }
    }
}
/* end of namespace declaration */
```

A C# program consists of statements, and each of these statements executes sequentially. In Listing 1-1 the Pow method, from the Math class, processes the square of a number, and the Write method, from the Console class, displays the processed square number on the console as output. When Listing 1-1 is compiled using the C# compiler csc.exe, and executes the executable, it will produce the output given here:

```
Original number        Square number
       0                    0
       1                    1
       2                    4
       3                    9
```

Listing 1-1 contains a class called a *program* inside the namespace Ch01. A *namespace* is used to organize classes, and *classes* are used to organize a group of function members, which is called a method. A *method* is a block of statement defined inside curly braces ({}), such as {statement list}, inside a class; for example:

```
static void Main( string[] args ){......}
```

The int literal 3 and the string literals "Original number" and "Square number" are used in the program to define three variables. In Listing 1-1 the iteration statement for is used to iterate through the processing. A local variable, i, is declared in the for loop as a loop variable. For more details on the compilation process of a C# program, see the section "Road Map to the CLR."

The C# language definition defines a machine-independent intermediate form known as common intermediate language (CIL), or IL code. IL code is the standard format for distribution of C# programs; it allows portable programs to be used in any environment that supports the CLR. The main C# compiler produces the IL code, which is then translated into machine code immediately prior to execution by the JIT compiler. CIL is deliberately language independent, so it can be used for code produced by a variety of front-end compilers. The C# language is different from traditional language (see Figure 1-8).

If you want to view the IL code, the front-end compiler generated for Listing 1-1 executes the following command at the Visual Studio command prompt:

```
J:\Book\C# Deconstructed\SourceCode\Chapters\CH_01\bin\Debug\>ildasm CH_01.exe /output:File.IL
```

This will produce, following the IL code, the Intermediate Language Disassembler (ILDASM) tool disassembly of the assembly.

// Microsoft (R) .NET Framework IL Disassembler Version 4.0.30319.1

```
// Copyright (c) Microsoft Corporation.  All rights reserved.

// Metadata version: v4.0.30319
.assembly extern mscorlib
{
  .publickeytoken = (B7 7A 5C 56 19 34 E0 89 )                 // .z\V.4..
  .ver 4:0:0:0
}
.assembly CH_01
{
  /*removed*/
  .hash algorithm 0x00008004
  .ver 1:0:0:0
}
.module CH_01.exe
// MVID: {B7A4D69C-5024-418E-9BDF-310A26522865}
.imagebase 0x00400000
.file alignment 0x00000200
.stackreserve 0x00100000
.subsystem 0x0003       // WINDOWS_CUI
.corflags 0x00000003    // ILONLY 32BITREQUIRED
// Image base: 0x002E0000
```

```
// =============== CLASS MEMBERS DECLARATION ===================

.class private auto ansi beforefieldinit Ch_01.Program
       extends [mscorlib]System.Object
{
  .method private hidebysig static void  Main(string[] args) cil managed
  {
    .entrypoint
    // Code size        15 (0xf)
    .maxstack  1
    .locals init ([0] class Ch_01.PowerGenerator pg)
    IL_0000:  nop
    IL_0001:  newobj      instance void Ch_01.PowerGenerator::.ctor()
    IL_0006:  stloc.0
    IL_0007:  ldloc.0
    IL_0008:  callvirt    instance void Ch_01.PowerGenerator::ProcessPower()
    IL_000d:  nop
    IL_000e:  ret
  } // end of method Program::Main

  .method public hidebysig specialname rtspecialname
          instance void   .ctor() cil managed
  {
    // Code size        7 (0x7)
    .maxstack  8
    IL_0000:  ldarg.0
    IL_0001:  call        instance void [mscorlib]System.Object::.ctor()
    IL_0006:  ret
  } // end of method Program::.ctor

} // end of class Ch_01.Program

.class public auto ansi beforefieldinit Ch_01.PowerGenerator
       extends [mscorlib]System.Object
{
  .field private static literal int32 limit = int32(0x00000003)
  .field private static literal string original = "Original number"
  .field private static literal string square = "Square number"
  .method public hidebysig instance void
          ProcessPower() cil managed
  {
    // Code size        82 (0x52)
    .maxstack  4
    .locals init ([0] int32 i,
             [1] bool CS$4$0000)
    IL_0000:  nop
    IL_0001:  ldstr       "{0,16}{1,20}"
    IL_0006:  ldstr       "Original number"
    IL_000b:  ldstr       "Square number"
    IL_0010:  call        void [mscorlib]System.Console::WriteLine(string,
                                                          object,
                                                          object)
```

```
    IL_0015:   nop
    IL_0016:   ldc.i4.0
    IL_0017:   stloc.0
    IL_0018:   br.s        IL_0046

    IL_001a:   nop
    IL_001b:   ldstr       "{0,10}{1,20}\n"
    IL_0020:   ldloc.0
    IL_0021:   box         [mscorlib]System.Int32
    IL_0026:   ldloc.0
    IL_0027:   conv.r8
    IL_0028:   ldc.r8      2.
    IL_0031:   call        float64 [mscorlib]System.Math::Pow(float64,
                                                              float64)
    IL_0036:   box         [mscorlib]System.Double
    IL_003b:   call        void [mscorlib]System.Console::Write(string,
                                                                object,
                                                                object)
    IL_0040:   nop
    IL_0041:   nop
    IL_0042:   ldloc.0
    IL_0043:   ldc.i4.1
    IL_0044:   add
    IL_0045:   stloc.0
    IL_0046:   ldloc.0
    IL_0047:   ldc.i4.3
    IL_0048:   cgt
    IL_004a:   ldc.i4.0
    IL_004b:   ceq
    IL_004d:   stloc.1
    IL_004e:   ldloc.1
    IL_004f:   brtrue.s    IL_001a

    IL_0051:   ret
  } // end of method PowerGenerator::ProcessPower

  .method public hidebysig specialname rtspecialname
          instance void  .ctor() cil managed
  {
    // Code size       7 (0x7)
    .maxstack  8
    IL_0000:   ldarg.0
    IL_0001:   call        instance void [mscorlib]System.Object::.ctor()
    IL_0006:   ret
  } // end of method PowerGenerator::.ctor

} // end of class Ch_01.PowerGenerator

// ============================================================

// ********** DISASSEMBLY COMPLETE **********************
// WARNING: Created Win32 resource file File.res
```

The CLR

In .NET the virtual execution system (VES) is known as the common language runtime (CLR). The CLR implements and enforces the common type system (CTS) model and is responsible for loading and running programs written for the common language infrastructure (CLI) (see Figure 1-9). The CLI provides the services needed to execute the managed code and data, using the metadata to connect separately generated modules at runtime (late binding). In this way, the CLI serves as a unifying framework for designing, developing, deploying, and executing distributed components and applications.

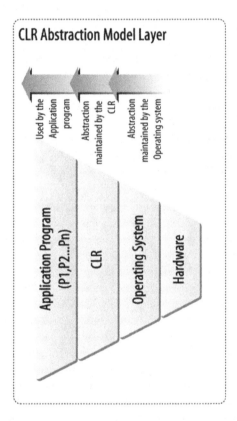

Figure 1-9. *CLR as a virtual execution environment*

The appropriate subset of the CTS is available from each programming language that targets the CLI. Language-based tools communicate with each other and with the VES, using metadata to define and reference the types used to construct the application. The VES uses the metadata to create instances of the types as needed and to give data type information to other parts of the infrastructure (such as remoting services, assembly downloading, and security).

The CLI supplies a specification for the CTS and metadata, the CLS, and the VES. Executable code is presented to the VES as modules. A module is a single file containing executable content in the format specified in Partition 2, sections 21–24 of the ECMA CLI standard, which is available on the ECMA web site (http://www.ecma-international.org/publications/standards/Ecma-335.htm).

The CLI's unified type system, CTS, is used by the compilers (C#, VB.NET, and so on), tools, and the CLI itself. The CLI supplies the model for defining the type in your application. This model includes the rules that CLI follows when declaring and managing types. The CTS is a rich type system that supports the types and operations of many programming languages (see Figure 1-10).

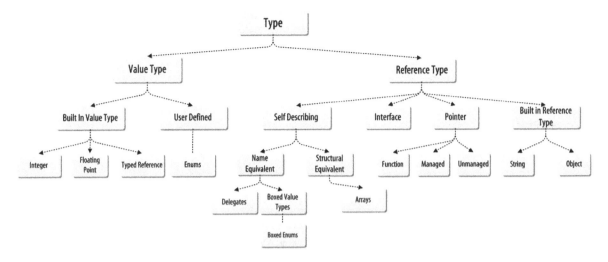

Figure 1-10. *CTS type system*

Details on the specification of the CTS and the complete list of CTS types can be found in Partition 1, section 8 of the ECMA CLI standard.

Road Map to the CLR

The C# compiler compiles the C# source code into the module, which is later converted into the assembly at the program's compile time. The *assembly* contains the IL code, along with the metadata concerning that assembly. The CLR works with the assembly, loading it and converting it into native code for execution.

When the CLR executes a program, it does so method by method. However, before the CLR executes any method, unless the method has already been JIT compiled, the CLR's JIT compiler needs to convert it into native code. The JIT compiler is responsible for compiling the IL code into native instructions for execution. The CLR retrieves the appropriate metadata concerning the method from the assembly, extracts the IL code for the method, and allocates a block of memory to the heap, where the JIT compiler will store the JITted native code for that method. Figure 1-11 demonstrates the compilation process of a C# program.

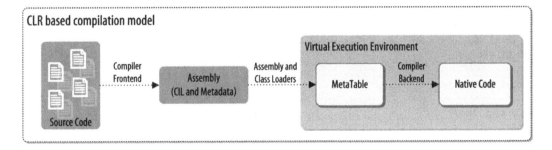

Figure 1-11. *Compilation overview*

An assembly is defined by a manifest, which is metadata that lists all the files included and directly referenced in the assembly, the types exported and imported by the assembly, versioning information, and security permissions that apply to the whole assembly.

```
using System;

namespace Ch_01
{
    class Program
    {
        static void Main(string[] args)
        {
            Console.Read();
            ClassTest ct = new ClassTest();
            while (true)
            {
                if (Console.ReadKey().Key == ConsoleKey.A)
                    break;
            }
        }
    }

    public class ClassTest
    {
        public void One() { }
        public void Two() { }
        public void Three() { }
    }
}
```

When this application is compiled into an assembly (Ch_01.exe), using csc.exe, you can view the contents of the assembly with the dumpbin tool, as shown:

```
J:\Book\C# Deconstructed\SourceCode\Chapters\CH_01\bin\Debug>dumpbin /all CH_01.exe>C:\CH_01_
Dumpbin.txt
```

The contents of the CH_01_Dumpbin.txt are as follows:

```
Microsoft (R) COFF/PE Dumper Version 10.00.30319.01
Copyright (C) Microsoft Corporation.  All rights reserved.


Dump of file CH_01.exe

PE signature found

File Type: EXECUTABLE IMAGE

FILE HEADER VALUES
            14C machine (x86)
              3 number of sections
       533D4124 time date stamp Thu Apr 03 22:08:20 2014
              0 file pointer to symbol table
              0 number of symbols
```

```
             E0 size of optional header
            102 characteristics
                   Executable
                   32 bit word machine

OPTIONAL HEADER VALUES
            10B magic # (PE32)
           8.00 linker version
            A00 size of code
            800 size of initialized data
              0 size of uninitialized data
           283E entry point (0040283E)
           2000 base of code
           4000 base of data
         400000 image base (00400000 to 00407FFF)
           2000 section alignment
            200 file alignment
           4.00 operating system version
           0.00 image version
           4.00 subsystem version
              0 Win32 version
           8000 size of image
            200 size of headers
              0 checksum
              3 subsystem (Windows CUI)
           8540 DLL characteristics
                   Dynamic base
                   NX compatible
                   No structured exception handler
                   Terminal Server Aware
         100000 size of stack reserve
           1000 size of stack commit
         100000 size of heap reserve
           1000 size of heap commit
              0 loader flags
             10 number of directories
              0 [       0] RVA [size] of Export Directory
           27F0 [      4B] RVA [size] of Import Directory
           4000 [     520] RVA [size] of Resource Directory
              0 [       0] RVA [size] of Exception Directory
              0 [       0] RVA [size] of Certificates Directory
           6000 [       C] RVA [size] of Base Relocation Directory
           2770 [      1C] RVA [size] of Debug Directory
              0 [       0] RVA [size] of Architecture Directory
              0 [       0] RVA [size] of Global Pointer Directory
              0 [       0] RVA [size] of Thread Storage Directory
              0 [       0] RVA [size] of Load Configuration Directory
              0 [       0] RVA [size] of Bound Import Directory
           2000 [       8] RVA [size] of Import Address Table Directory
              0 [       0] RVA [size] of Delay Import Directory
           2008 [      48] RVA [size] of COM Descriptor Directory
              0 [       0] RVA [size] of Reserved Directory
```

```
SECTION HEADER #1
    .text name
      844 virtual size
     2000 virtual address (00402000 to 00402843)
      A00 size of raw data
      200 file pointer to raw data (00000200 to 00000BFF)
        0 file pointer to relocation table
        0 file pointer to line numbers
        0 number of relocations
        0 number of line numbers
 60000020 flags
          Code
          Execute Read

RAW DATA #1
  00402000: 40 28 00 00 00 00 00 00 48 00 00 00 02 00 05 00   @(......H.......
  00402010: A8 20 00 00 04 07 00 00 03 00 00 00 01 00 00 06   ¨ .............

 /* removed */

  00402840: 00 00 5F 43 6F 72 45 78 65 4D 61 69 6E 00 6D 73   .._CorExeMain.ms
  00402850: 63 6F 72 65 65 2E 64 6C 6C 00 00 00 00 00 FF 25   coree.dll.....ÿ%
  00402860: 00 20 40 00                                       . @.

    Debug Directories

        Time Type         Size      RVA  Pointer
     -------- ------   --------  -------- --------
     533D4124 cv             63 0000278C      98C    Format: RSDS, {ABA92538-B058-4C6C-AFA8-
2208F3586205}, 3, J:\Book\C# Deconstructed\SourceCode\Chapters\CH_01\obj\x86\Debug\CH_01.pdb

    clr Header:

              48 cb
            2.05 runtime version
            20A8 [      6C8] RVA [size] of MetaData Directory
               3 flags
                   IL Only
                   32-Bit Required
         6000001 entry point token
               0 [        0] RVA [size] of Resources Directory
               0 [        0] RVA [size] of StrongNameSignature Directory
               0 [        0] RVA [size] of CodeManagerTable Directory
               0 [        0] RVA [size] of VTableFixups Directory
               0 [        0] RVA [size] of ExportAddressTableJumps Directory
               0 [        0] RVA [size] of ManagedNativeHeader Directory
```

    Section contains the following imports:

      mscoree.dll
                    402000 Import Address Table
                    402818 Import Name Table
                         0 time date stamp
                         0 Index of first forwarder reference

                         0 _CorExeMain

SECTION HEADER #2
     .rsrc name
       520 virtual size
      4000 virtual address (00404000 to 0040451F)
       600 size of raw data
       C00 file pointer to raw data (00000C00 to 000011FF)
         0 file pointer to relocation table
         0 file pointer to line numbers
         0 number of relocations
         0 number of line numbers
  40000040 flags
           Initialized Data
           Read Only

RAW DATA #2
  00404000: 00 00 00 00 00 00 00 00 00 00 00 00 00 00 02 00 ....
/* removed */
  004045B0: 66 6F 3E 0D 0A 3C 2F 61 73 73 65 6D 62 6C 79 3E fo>..</assembly>
  004045C0: 0D 0A 00 00 00 00 00 00   ....

SECTION HEADER #3
    .reloc name
         C virtual size
      6000 virtual address (00406000 to 0040600B)
       200 size of raw data
      1200 file pointer to raw data (00001200 to 000013FF)
         0 file pointer to relocation table
         0 file pointer to line numbers
         0 number of relocations
         0 number of line numbers
  42000040 flags
           Initialized Data
           Discardable
           Read Only

RAW DATA #3
  00406000: 00 20 00 00 0C 00 00 00 60 38 00 00   . ...`8..

```
BASE RELOCATIONS #3
    2000 RVA,        C SizeOfBlock
     860  HIGHLOW            00402000
       0  ABS

  Summary

        2000 .reloc
        2000 .rsrc
        2000 .text
```

Tools Used in This Book

WinDbg is a debugging tool for performing user and kernel-mode debugging. This tool comes from Microsoft, as part of the Windows Driver Kit (WDK). WinDbg is a *graphical user interface GUI)* built on Console Debugger (CDB), NT Symbolic Debugger (NTSD), and kernel debugging, along with debugging extensions. The Son of Strike (SOS) debugging extension DLL (dynamic link library) helps debug managed assembly by providing information on the internal CLR environment.

WinDbg is a powerful tool; it can be used to debug managed assembly. and it allows you to set a breakpoint; view source code, using symbol files; view stack trace information; view heap information; see the parameters of a method, a memory, and registers; examine exception handling information; and much more.

WinDbg comes as part of the Debugging Tools for Windows package; WinDbg is free and available on the Microsoft Web site (http://msdn.microsoft.com/en-us/windows/hardware/gg463009.aspx). Once you have downloaded and installed the installation package, open WinDbg from the installed directory, for example, by going to Programs ➤ Debugging Tools for Windows (x86) ➤ WinDbg.

A symbol file contains variety of data that can be used in the debugging process, but this information is not necessary for running the binaries.

Symbol files may contain

- Global variables

- Local variables

- Function names and the addresses of their entry points

- Frame pointer omission (FPO) records

- Source line numbers

When the debugger tools (such as WinDbg) have to have access to the related symbol files, then you need to set the symbol file location. Microsoft has provided a symbol server, so it is good to point the debugger to it. To do this, you can use the srv command, along with the local cached folder, to which the symbol files will be downloaded, and the server location, from which the symbol files will be downloaded. It is as simple to use the symbol server with the srv command as it is to use the appropriate syntax in your symbol path. Typically, the syntax takes the following format:

```
SRV*your local cached folder*http://msdl.microsoft.com/download/symbols
```

The local cached folder should contain any drive or share that is used as a symbol destination. For instance, to set the symbol path in WinDbg, type this command in the Command window of the debugger:

```
.sympath SRV*C:\symbols*http://msdl.microsoft.com/download/symbols
```

In the Symbol Search Path window, the symbol path location has been set as shown:

```
SRV*c:\symbols*http://msdl.microsoft.com/download/symbols
```

Here, `c:\symbols` refers to the local cached folder, to which the symbol file will be downloaded from the location specified as `http://msdl.microsoft.com/download/symbols`.

The final, important step of the WinDbg setup is to use right version of the SOS debugging extension DLL. You will learn about this in the following section.

Son of Strike Debugging Extension DLL

The Son of Strike (SOS) debugging extension DLL helps debug managed assembly. 4With SOS, you will be able to

- Display managed call stacks

- Set breakpoints in managed code

- Find the values of local variables

- Dump the arguments to method calls

- Perform most of the inspection and control debugging actions that you can use in native-code debugging—only without the convenience of source level debugging

To load `SOS.dll` and initiate the debugging environment in WinDbg, you need to run the following commands:

```
sxe ld clrjit
g
.loadby sos clr
.load sos.dll
```

The `.load sos.dll` command is used to load SOS, but if WinDbg cannot find the right version of the SOS, it throws exception.

In .NET every version of the CLR has its own copy of the SOS extension DLL. You must always make sure to load the right version of the SOS. To do this, you need to use the full path of the SOS (installed in your system), using the `.load` command. The path syntax is asfollows:

```
.load <full path to sos.dll>
```

Or, altermatively:

```
.load %windir%\Microsoft.NET\Framework\<version>\sos.dll
```

For example, if the SOS is installed in the `C:\Windows\Microsoft.NET\Framework\v4.0.30319\` directory, you may need to execute this command:

```
.load C:\Windows\Microsoft.NET\Framework\v4.0.30319\sos.dll
```

The complete list of the commands is as shown:

```
sxe ld clrjit
g
.loadby sos clr
.load C:\Windows\Microsoft.NET\Framework\v4.0.30319\sos.dll
```

The ILDASM tool uses to examine .NET Framework assemblies in IL format, such as `mscorlib.dll`, as well as other .NET Framework assemblies provided by a third party or created by you. The ILDASM parses any .NET Framework–managed assembly. ILDASM can be used to

- Explore Microsoft intermediate language (MSIL) code

- Displays namespaces and types, including their interfaces

- Examine the executable header information

The ILDASM tool comes with.NET Framework Software Development Kit (SDK), so you don't need to download; it will be installed as part of the Visual Studio installation.

Conclusion

A basic computer system consists of three main components: CPU, physical memory, and I/O. The CPU is the core component, running the system, using the instructions it has defined and stored in the microcode component. This instruction set has been abstracted into a high level to make the computer system closer to the people who program. This was possible by introducing the concept of high-level programming language, with the help of a piece of software called the compiler. The compiler concept became more dynamic with the introduction of the JIT compiler. In C# language the JIT compiler is used to compile the language that targets the virtual execution environment, such as CLR.

The CLR is a virtual execution environment. In layperson's terms, the CLR is an abstraction of the execution environment of an OS for the application program. You will learn about the virtual execution environment in Chapter 2. The CLR understands the language it supports, such as IL. To execute any application program in .NET with the CLR, a mechanism called the assembly is used to package the source code and pass it into the CLR to execute. You will explore the assembly in Chapter 3.

As you have already seen, the CPU fetches application instructions from physical memory. It is crucial to know how memory works and is managed by the OS. Most importantl you should know how the CLR uses this memory to implement its own memory model. You will learn about memory management in the OS and CLR in Chapters 4 and 5.

So far, you have seen how the C# application is compiled by the front-end compiler and packaged into a construct called the assembly. The assembly is loaded into and laid out in the physical memory and executed by the CPU. But, owing to virtual execution, the CPU and OS will not be able to execute the assembly simply by fetching it from the memory. The execution model of the CLR takes care of this. You will learn about the execution model of the CLR in Chapters 6 and 7.

Further Reading

Bryant, Randal E., and David R. O'Hallaron. *Computer Systems: A Programmer's Perspective* Upper Saddle River, NJ: Prentice Hall, 2003.

Hyde, Randall. *The Art of Assembly Language*. San Francisco: No Starch, 2003.

Hyde, Randall. *Write Great Code*. Vol. 2, *Writing High Level*. San Francisco: No Starch, 2006.

Miller, James S., and Susann Ragsdale, S). *The Common Language Infrastructure Annotated Standard*. Boston: Addison-Wesley, 2004.

Murdocca, Miles J., and Vincent P. Heuring. *Principles of Computer Architecture*. Upper Saddle River, NJ: Prentice Hall, 2000.

Scott, Michael L. *Programming Language Pragmatics*. San Francisco: Morgan Kaufmann, 2000.

Sebesta, Robert W. *Concepts of Programming Languages, Fifth Edition*. Boston: Addison-Wesley, 2002.

Stokes, Jon. *Inside the Machine: An Illustrated Introduction to Microprocessors and Computer Architecture*. San Francisco: No Starch, 2007.

CHAPTER 2

■ ■ ■

The Virtual Machine and CLR

A virtual machine is a virtual computer system that runs on the existing OS, or the host OS. A virtual machine provides virtual hardware to the OS that targets the virtual machine. This is sometimes referred to as the guest OS.

Virtual machine systems were originally introduced to overcome some of the shortcomings of the existing computer system. This virtual machine concept was adapted to the area of programming language by introducing the virtual execution environment. In this chapter, you will learn about the virtual machine. Then, you will explore the virtual execution environment, such as the CLR, which is Microsoft's implementation of the virtual execution environment, targeting .NET languages.

Virtual Machine

The term *virtual* can denote a technology that is used in the computer world. This technology is implemented as software that runs on top of the OS and hardware. This virtualization concept has brought huge advancements to computer system architecture. The virtual machine has helped decouple hardware and software design, such that hardware and software designer can work more or less independently. The application developer can concentrate on the application side without worrying about the changes to the OS, and hardware and software can be upgraded according to different schedules. Most important, software can run on different hardware platforms targeting different ISA. To begin, let's see why we need a virtual environment.

Problems with the Existing System

In traditional computer architecture the major components of a computer system are the application program, the OS, and the hardware. These components can work only when they are in harmony. For example, Microsoft has built an application for its Office suite targeting the Windows OS for the x86 platform; thus, this application can run solely when it is in this environment. Similarly, Linux applications built targeting the Linux OS can run only on the Linux OS, Macintosh applications built for the Macintosh OS will not run on Windows, and Windows applications built for Windows will not execute on the Linux platform. This is one of the fundamental problems in typical computer architecture (see Figure 2-1).

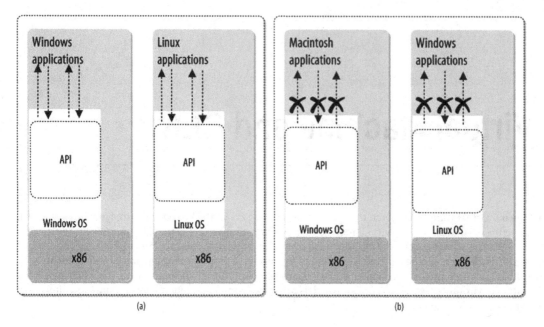

Figure 2-1. *Existing problems with the traditional computer system*

If you look closely at this problem, you will find that application software compiled for a particular ISA will not run on a hardware platform that implements a different ISA. For instance, Macintosh application binaries will not directly execute on an Intel processor. Likewise, Windows applications built for the x86 hardware will not be able to execute on a platform other than the x86. Even if the underlying ISA is the same, applications compiled for one OS will not run if a different OS is used. For example, applications compiled for Linux and for Windows use different system calls, so a Windows application cannot run directly on a Linux system, and vice versa.

Optimization During Execution

As an application developer, you must be aware of the optimization and performance of your application. An application whose code is optimized for a certain hardware platform will perform well only when it is executed by that platform. When you compile an application using a compiler, the compiler may produce optimized executable code, based on your underlying hardware (CPU), but if you take that executable to a different hardware platform, your application may struggle to perform well, owing to the optimization issue. Typically, only one version of a binary is distributed, and it is likely optimized for only one processor model (if it is optimized at all). To address these problems, special coupling software can be used to connect the major components, as shown in Figure 2-2.

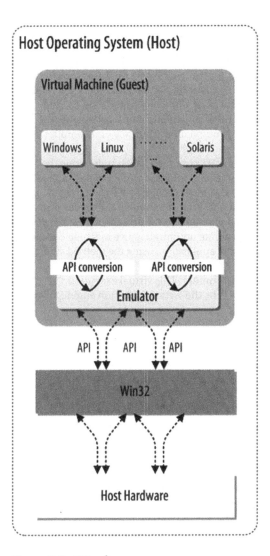

Figure 2-2. *VM software*

The coupling software shown in the figure 2is called Virtual Machine (VM). It is used to connect the guest application with the host OS. Using its emulator component, VM translates the ISA, such that the conventional software sees one ISA, while the hardware supports another.

The concept of the virtual machine has a huge portability value for any program targeted by the virtual machine. The virtual machine will execute the targeted program, regardless of the underlying hardware platform, translating it based on that platform. This portability raises the possibility of creating a virtual execution environment that supports execution of the program code. In the following sections, you will learn about the virtual execution environment.

Virtual Execution Environment

The virtual execution environment plays an important role in the optimization and portability of application programs. The virtual execution environment introduces the concept of IL (for the .NET platform, IL; for Java, byte code; and so on). The languages that target the virtual machine (for the .NET platform, C#, VB.NET, and so on) will be compiled into this intermediate code at compile time. This compilation process is sometimes referred to as front-end compilation. At runtime or execution time the intermediate code will be compiled into native code, using the JIT compiler. In this book I will sometimes refer to this process as back-end compilation. The back-end compiler will produce optimized native code targeting the underlying CPU.

The virtual execution environment also has the capability to execute the JIT compiled native code, using the OS services. Here, *virtual execution* denotes the circumstance in which an application program written and compiled using the languages supported by the virtual machine is executed, managed, and controlled by the same virtual machine. For example, the virtual machine may handle memory management services; maintain the execution state, using the concept of the method state; communicate with the OS to get the schedule for the processes running; and so on. A virtual machine, such as Microsoft's CLR, uses the JIT compiler to generate optimized native machine code from the intermediate code at runtime; manages and controls the execution of the application, using the method state; manages the object life cycle, using the GC; and so on.

Figure 2-3 illustrates a model of a hypothetical virtual execution environment. This virtual execution environment controls and manages the execution of the languages L1 to Ln by the virtual execution engine, using the underlying OS's services.

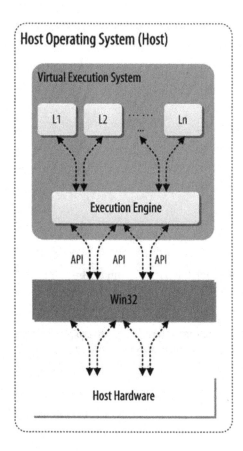

Figure 2-3. A typical VES

Components of the Virtual Execution Environment

A typical virtual execution environment has one or more programming languages, compiled into an IL form, that will execute on that virtual platform. *Virtual execution* means that the compiled program will be executed by the underlying OS but that the virtual machine will have all the control in managing the execution. The virtual execution environment provides a layer of abstraction between a compiled program and the underlying OS and hardware platform. Figure 2-4 displays a typical virtual execution environment.

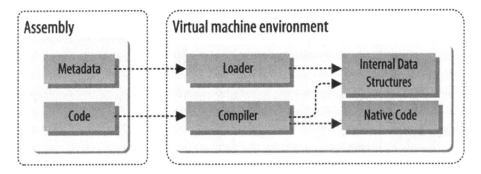

Figure 2-4. *High-level overview of the VES*

An assembly consists of platform-independent code and platform-independent metadata. The metadata describe the data structures (typically objects), their attributes, and their relationships. As shown in the figure, the VM software consists of an emulator that can either interpret the code or translate it into native code. For example, in C# language, IL code is compiled into native code, using the JIT compiler of the CLR. In this book, you will learn how the CLR executes and uses CLI to generate the native code to run on a native machine. You will also discover some of CLR's advantages, namely, portability, compactness, efficiency, security, interoperability, flexibility, and, above all, multi language support.

CLR: Virtual Machine for .NET

The CLR is the Microsoft implementation of the virtual execution environment. The CLR manages the execution of source code written using C#, VB.NET, or any other language supported by .NET. The source code is first compiled into MSIL, and later, during the execution phase, it is compiled into native code.

The CLR offers many services, such as code management; software memory isolation; loading and execution of managed assembly; and compilation of the IL code into native code, including verification of the type safety of the MSIL code. The CLR also accesses the metadata embedded within the assembly to lay out the type information in memory and provides memory management, using the GC. In addition, the CLR handles exceptions, including cross-language exceptions.

CLR SPECIFICATION

The ECMA C# and CLI standards can be downloaded from the Microsoft web site (http://msdn.microsoft.com/en-us/vstudio/aa569283.aspx),

---

Figure 2-5 gives a high-level view of the CLR. The source code targeting the CLR is compiled into the IL and assembled in the assembly. The assembly resides in the storage device (typically found on the hard drive) and contains IL code and metadata. Before the assembly's execution, the CLR loads it into memory and compiles the relevant IL code into native code. The assembly is then executed by the underlying OS.

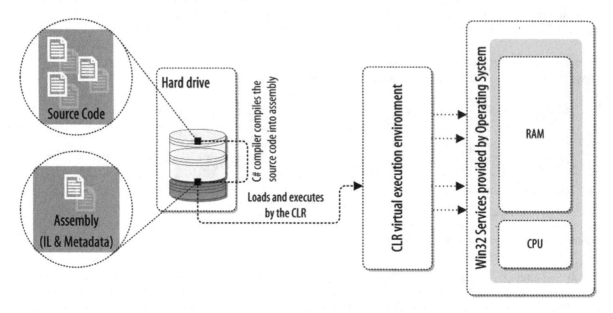

Figure 2-5. *The internal CLR execution environment*

The CLR provides private virtual address space for each of the applications it executes. The address space uses mechanism called the application domain to afford the software isolation for the running applications. The CLR enforces type safety access to all areas of memory when running type-safe managed code.

The CLR supplies the common infrastructure that allows tools and programming languages to benefit from cross-language integration. Any technical improvements to the CLR will be of help to all languages and tools that target the .NET Framework.

CLR Supports Multiple Languages

The CLR has advantages: it supports multiple languages and targets many platforms. Figure 2-6 shows the C#, F#, VB.NET, J#, and Managed C++ languages compiled into the assembly, which contains simply IL code and metadata. The assembly targets the CLR, which serves as a middle layer between the compiled code and the underlying OS.

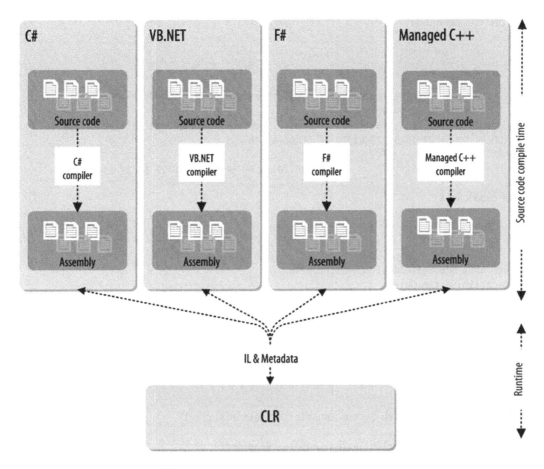

Figure 2-6. *CLR and multiple languages*

The following four programs, written accordingly, using C#, Managed C++, F#, and VB.NET, respectively, compile type at the front-end and will produce CLR-understandable IL code.

C# source code and disassembled IL code:

```
//Program.cs
using System;

namespace Ch_01
{

    class Program
    {

        static void Main(string[] args)
        {
            Console.WriteLine("C#");
            Console.ReadLine();
        }
    }
}
```

IL code for the previous assembly:

```
/*removed*/
.assembly Program
{
  .custom instance void [mscorlib]System.Runtime.CompilerServices.CompilationRelaxationsAttribute::
  .ctor(int32) = ( 01 00 08 00 00 00 00 00 )
  .custom instance void [mscorlib]System.Runtime.CompilerServices.RuntimeCompatibilityAttribute::
  .ctor() = ( 01 00 01 00 54 02 16 57 72 61 70 4E 6F 6E 45 78
// ....T..WrapNonEx
                                          63 65 70 74 69 6F 6E 54 68 72 6F 77 73 01 )
// ceptionThrows.
  .hash algorithm 0x00008004
  .ver 0:0:0:0
}
/*removed*/

.class private auto ansi beforefieldinit Ch_01.Program
       extends [mscorlib]System.Object
{
  .method private hidebysig static void  Main(string[] args) cil managed
  {
    .entrypoint
    // Code size       19 (0x13)
    .maxstack  8
    IL_0000: nop
    IL_0001: ldstr      "C#"
    IL_0006: call       void [mscorlib]System.Console::WriteLine(string)
    IL_000b: nop
    IL_000c: call       string [mscorlib]System.Console::ReadLine()
    IL_0011: pop
    IL_0012: ret
  } // end of method Program::Main
/*removed*/

// ********** DISASSEMBLY COMPLETE ***********************
// WARNING: Created Win32 resource file Program.res
```

Managed C++ source code and disassembled IL code:

```
// FileName: ManagedCPlusPlus.cpp
#include "stdafx.h"

using namespace System;

int main(array<System::String ^> ^args)
{
    Console::WriteLine(L"Managed C++");
               Console::ReadLine();
    return 0;
}
```

IL code for the prior assembly:

```
/*removed*/
.assembly ManagedCPlusPlus
{
  .custom instance void [mscorlib]System.Security.SecurityRulesAttribute::.ctor
(valuetype [mscorlib]System.Security.SecurityRuleSet) = ( 01 00 01 00 00 )
  .permissionset reqmin
           = {[mscorlib]System.Security.Permissions.SecurityPermissionAttribute =
{property bool 'SkipVerification' = bool(true)}}
  .hash algorithm 0x00008004
  .ver 0:0:0:0
}
/*removed*/

.method assembly static int32  main(string[] args) cil managed
{
  // Code size       22 (0x16)
  .maxstack  1
 .locals (int32 V_0)
  IL_0000: ldc.i4.0
  IL_0001: stloc.0
  IL_0002: ldstr      "Managed C++"
  IL_0007: call       void [mscorlib]System.Console::WriteLine(string)
  IL_000c: call       string [mscorlib]System.Console::ReadLine()
  IL_0011: pop
  IL_0012: ldc.i4.0
  IL_0013: stloc.0
  IL_0014: ldloc.0
  IL_0015: ret
} // end of global method main

/*removed*/
// ********** DISASSEMBLY COMPLETE **********************
```

F# source code and disassembled IL code:

```
//FileName: FSharpProgram.fs
System.Console.WriteLine("F#\n Press any key to continue")
System.Console.ReadLine()
```

IL code for the previous assembly:

```
/*removed*/
.assembly FSharpProgram
{
  .custom instance void [FSharp.Core]Microsoft.FSharp.Core.FSharpInterfaceDataVersionAttribute::
  .ctor(int32,
               int32,
               int32) = ( 01 00 02 00 00 00 00 00 00 00 00 00 00 00 00 00
)
  .hash algorithm 0x00008004
  .ver 0:0:0:0
}
/*removed*/

.class private abstract auto ansi sealed '<StartupCode$FSharpProgram>'.$FSharpProgram
       extends [mscorlib]System.Object
{
  .field static assembly int32 init@
  .custom instance void [mscorlib]System.Diagnostics.DebuggerBrowsableAttribute::.ctor(valuetype
  [mscorlib]System.Diagnostics.DebuggerBrowsableState) = ( 01 00 00 00 00 00 00 00 )
  .custom instance void [mscorlib]System.Runtime.CompilerServices.CompilerGeneratedAttribute::
  .ctor() = ( 01 00 00 00 )
  .custom instance void [mscorlib]System.Diagnostics.DebuggerNonUserCodeAttribute::
  .ctor() = ( 01 00 00 00 )
  .method public static void main@() cil managed
  {
    .entrypoint
    // Code size        17 (0x11)
    .maxstack  3
    IL_0000: ldstr      "F#\n Press any key to continue"
    IL_0005: call       void [mscorlib]System.Console::WriteLine(string)
    IL_000a: call       string [mscorlib]System.Console::ReadLine()
    IL_000f: pop
    IL_0010: ret
  } // end of method $FSharpProgram::main@

} // end of class '<StartupCode$FSharpProgram>'.$FSharpProgram


// =============================================================

// ********** DISASSEMBLY COMPLETE ***********************
// WARNING: Created Win32 resource file FSharpProgram.res
```

VB.NET source code and disassembled IL code:

```
//FileName: MainModule.vb
Module MainModule

    Sub Main()
        Console.WriteLine("VB.NET")
    End Sub

End Module
```

IL code for the prior assembly:

```
/*removed*/
.assembly MainModule
{
  .custom instance void [mscorlib]System.Runtime.CompilerServices.RuntimeCompatibilityAttribute::
  .ctor() = ( 01 00 01 00 54 02 16 57 72 61 70 4E 6F 6E 45 78
// ....T..WrapNonEx

63 65 70 74 69 6F 6E 54 68 72 6F 77 73 01 )
// ceptionThrows.
  .custom instance void [mscorlib]System.Runtime.CompilerServices.CompilationRelaxationsAttribute::
  .ctor(int32) = ( 01 00 08 00 00 00 00 00 )
  .hash algorithm 0x00008004
  .ver 0:0:0:0
}
/*removed*/

.class private auto ansi sealed MainModule
       extends [mscorlib]System.Object
{
  .custom instance void [Microsoft.VisualBasic]Microsoft.VisualBasic.CompilerServices.
   StandardModuleAttribute::.ctor() = ( 01 00 00 00 )
  .method public static void  Main() cil managed
  {
    .entrypoint
    .custom instance void [mscorlib]System.STAThreadAttribute::.ctor() = ( 01 00 00 00 )
    // Code size       11 (0xb)
    .maxstack  8
    IL_0000: ldstr      "VB.NET"
    IL_0005: call       void [mscorlib]System.Console::WriteLine(string)
    IL_000a: ret
  } // end of method MainModule::Main

} // end of class MainModule


// =================================================================

// ********** DISASSEMBLY COMPLETE ***********************
// WARNING: Created Win32 resource file MainModule.res
```

COMPILERS AND ILDASM

For C#, Managed C++, F#, and VB.NET, the respective commands are as follows:

```
csc.exe Program.cs
cl /clr ManagedCPlusPlus.cpp
fsc.exe FSharpProgram.fs
vbc /reference:Microsoft.VisualBasic.dll MainModule.vb
```

To disassemble the assembly, use the following `ildasm` commands accordingly for C#, Managed C++, F#, and VB.NET code:

```
ildasm Program.exe /out:Program.il
ildasm ManagedCPlusPlus.exe /out:ManagedCPlusPlus.il
ildasm FSharpProgram.exe /out:FSharpProgram.il
ildasm MainModule.exe /out:MainModule.il
```

A .NET application written in any of the .NET-supported languages is compiled into IL code, which is in turn JIT compiled at runtime into native code. The JIT compiler can produce optimized native code, based on the underlying hardware.

Common Components of the CLR

As mentioned earlier, the CLR is the implementation of the CLI. The architecture of CLI comprises the following elements:

- CTS
- CLS
- CIL instruction set
- VES (executes managed code and lies between code and the native OS)

The CTS defines the complete set of types available to a CLI-compliant program. In contrast, CLS defines the subset of CTS types that can be used for external calls. Using the metadata concerning the code and data, the CLR identifies the locations of objects and gives this information to the VES, which handles all the major overheads of traditional programming models (exceptions, security concerns, performance, pointers, object life cycle, and so on).

CIL is an assembly-like language that is generated by the compilers of languages targeting CLI. How and when the CIL is compiled to machine code is not specified by the standard, and those determinations rest with the implementation of the VES. The most frequently used model is employment of a JIT compiler, which generates native code as needed. Install-time compilers are another option, and it is also possible to implement an interpreter rather than a compiler for the CIL.

A typical .NET virtual machine

- Executes code at runtime
- Manages the execution by maintaining the state
- Manages objects
- Isolates address space, and so on (see Chapter X)

Conclusion

The CLR is the Microsoft implementation of the virtual execution environment. The CLR supports multiple languages, such as C#, VB.NET, and F#. If you write an application program using any of the CLR-supported languages, you will be able to execute the compiled version of your application via the CLR. When you compile your .NET application. the compiler compiles IL code and metadata. The compiler also uses a mechanism called the assembly to package the IL code and metadata. In .NET the assembly is a deployment mechanism of your application program. The assembly is loaded into memory and executed by the CLR. Therefore, it is important to understand how the assembly is structured by the compiler, what this assembly contains, and how the CLR lays it out in memory.

In the next chapter, you will explore the assembly and its structure as well as the assembly-loading process used in the CLR.

Further Reading

Juola, Patrick. *Principles of Computer Organization and Assembly Language*. Upper Saddle River, NJ: Prentice Hall, 2007.

Smith, James E., and Ravi Nair. *Virtual Machines: Versatile Platforms for Systems and Processes*. Amsterdam: Morgan Kaufmann, 2005.

Stokes, Jon. *Inside the Machine: An Illustrated Introduction to Microprocessors and Computer Architecture*. San Francisco: No Starch, 2007.

CHAPTER 3

■ ■ ■

Assembly

Assembly is a technical term used in the CLI to define a deployment unit. An assembly is a collection of compiled code, presented as module and resources files, that forms a logical unit of functionality for deployment, versioning, reuse, and security. In this chapter, you will learn about the assembly.

What Is the Assembly?

In .NET Framework an assembly exists in two forms: executable (EXE) and dynamic link library (DLL). Assemblies such as `mscorlib.dll`, `System.dll`, and `System.Configuration.dll` are the DLL forms of assembly used in .NET framework. Executable produced by the C# compiler (`csc.exe`) is a form of EXE assembly (see Listing 3-1). Assemblies targeting the CLI contain code in CIL. The CIL is usually generated from a CLI language, such as C# or VB.NET, and at runtime is compiled into native code by the JIT compiler.

An assembly always contains a manifest that specifies

- Version, name, culture, and security requirements for the assembly.

- Which other files, if any, belong to the assembly, along with a cryptographic hash of each file; the manifest itself resides in the metadata part of a file, and that file is always part of the assembly.

- The types defined in other files of the assembly that it is to export; types defined in the same file as the manifest are exported based on attributes of the type itself.

- Optionally, a digital signature for the manifest itself and the public key used to compute it.

Here is an example of a manifest, extracted from Listing 3-1:

```
// Metadata version: v4.0.30319
.assembly extern mscorlib
{ .publickeytoken = (B7 7A 5C 56 19 34 E0 89 )
  .ver 4:0:0:0
}
.assembly extern System.Core
{ .publickeytoken = (B7 7A 5C 56 19 34 E0 89 )
  .ver 4:0:0:0
}
.assembly extern System.Management
{ .publickeytoken = (B0 3F 5F 7F 11 D5 0A 3A )
  .ver 4:0:0:0
}
```

```
.assembly DassemblyConsole
{ /*reference to the other types*/
  /* Hash code */
  .hash algorithm 0x00008004
  .ver 1:0:0:0
}
.module DassemblyConsole.exe
// MVID: {332DA5EA-B803-42A6-8DDF-B27D1E92D6D3}
.imagebase 0x00400000
.file alignment 0x00000200
.stackreserve 0x00100000
.subsystem 0x0003       // WINDOWS_CUI
.corflags 0x00000003    // ILONLY 32BITREQUIRED
// Image base: 0x03260000
```

In this chapter, you will explore the assembly, including its structure, (based on Partition 2 of the ECMA C# standard) and how the CLR loads it at runtime. First, you will get an overview, using a simple C# application to examine compilation by the C# compiler and to see a hexadecimal formatted view of the compiled assembly contents. Then, you will analyze the hexadecimal contents to get a better understanding of assembly structure. Finally, you will discover how the assembly is loaded by the assembly-loader component of the CLR.

CLI SPECIFICATION

The ECMA CLI standard can be downloaded from the ECMA web site:

http://www.ecma-international.org/publications/standards/Ecma-335.htm

---

Overview of Modules, Assemblies, and Files

Once a program and its associated types are written as a form of source code, and that code is compiled into an assembly, the resulting assembly is distributed for use directly by user application (EXE) or indirectly by libraries (DLL), which depend on its exported library types and functions. As mentioned earlier, the CLR's logical unit of deployment, execution, and reuse is, in this case, the assembly. An assembly contains one-to-many smaller, independent physical units, or modules. Modules are files that are logically part of their containing assembly. Modules can contain not only managed metadata and code, but also ordinary files, such as localized resources, plain text, and opaque binary. The vast majority of managed applications employ single-file assemblies (i.e., those with one module), although the ability to create multifile assemblies is a powerful (and underused) capability. Figure 3-1 demonstrates this general architecture at a high level.

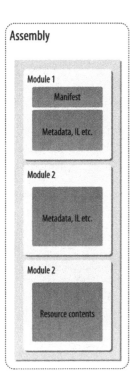

***Figure 3-1.** A typical assembly structure*

Introduction to PE Files

A portable executable (PE) is a file that is executable by the Windows OS. A PE file generally has an `.exe` or a `.dll` extension. The first bytes in a PE file form a header, which can be interpreted by Windows when the executable is launched. These bytes contain information such as the earliest version of Windows with which the executable can be used and if the executable is a GUI or console application. The format of a PE file is optimized so as not to degrade performance. Except for a few bytes, the rest of the file is an image of how the executable will be stored in memory. Modules are also PE files, as the .NET platform takes advantage of Windows services to execute applications. (Moreover, common object file format (PE/COFF) is the format used by the C++ compiler when it links object files. The COFF extension of the PE/COFF format is ignored by the.NET platform.

The specification of the C# assembly has been defined in Partition 2 of the ECMA C# standard. Based on the specification rule defined in clause 25.1, a typical assembly is structured as shown in Figure 3-2.

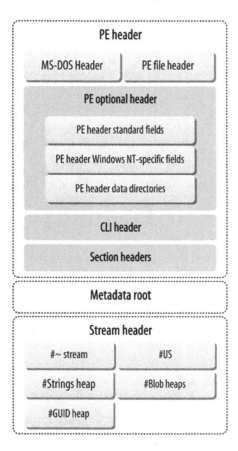

Figure 3-2. *Structure of the PE file*

As you can see, a PE executable, or image, starts with the MS-DOS header, which is predefined as a 128-byte MS-DOS stub placed at the front of the module. MS-DOS js followed by a PE signature and then the PE file header. The PE file header is 18 bytes of data used to define information such as the number of sections used in the image, the number of symbol tables, and so on. The PE optional header comes next. It is used to define the most importantly to the data directories. The PE optional header is followed by PE section headers. The PE section table contains a number of PE section headers, each of which has a total of 40 bytes of data.

Structure of the Assembly

Now, you will use the C# program depicted in Listing 3-1 to advance your understanding of assembly structure:

Listing 3-1.

```
using System;

namespace CH_03
{
    class Program
    {
        static void Main(string[] args)
```

```
        {
            Book book = new Book();
            book.Print();
        }
    }
    public class Book
    {
        public void Print() { Console.WriteLine("Blue Sky."); }
    }
}
```

This program was compiled using the C# compiler, which generates the executable for the program. You will open the executable with the HxD tool (or, you can choose your favorite hexadecimal viewer) to get the executable file contents as hexadecimal format. Later in the chapter, I will be using this hexadecimal output to discuss the structure of the assembly.

```
Offset(h) 00 01 02 03 04 05 06 07 08 09 0A 0B 0C 0D 0E 0F
00000000  4D 5A 90 00 03 00 00 00 04 00 00 00 FF FF 00 00  MZ.........ÿÿ..
00000010  B8 00 00 00 00 00 00 00 40 00 00 00 00 00 00 00  ¸.......@.......
00000020  00 00 00 00 00 00 00 00 00 00 00 00 00 00 00 00  ................
00000030  00 00 00 00 00 00 00 00 00 00 00 00 80 00 00 00  ............€...
00000040  0E 1F BA 0E 00 B4 09 CD 21 B8 01 4C CD 21 54 68  ..º..´.Í!¸.LÍ!Th
00000050  69 73 20 70 72 6F 67 72 61 6D 20 63 61 6E 6E 6F  is program canno
00000060  74 20 62 65 20 72 75 6E 20 69 6E 20 44 4F 53 20  t be run in DOS
00000070  6D 6F 64 65 2E 0D 0D 0A 24 00 00 00 00 00 00 00  mode....$.......

00000080  50 45 00 00                                      PE..
```

```
/*PE file header*/
                    4C 01 03 00 A5 0D 2D 53 00 00 00 00  PE..L...¥.-S....
00000090  00 00 00 00 E0 00 02 01                          ....à...
```

```
/* PE header standard fields */
                    0B 01 08 00 00 08 00 00  ....à...........
000000A0  00 08 00 00 00 00 00 00 BE 27 00 00 00 20 00 00  ........¾'... ..
000000B0  00 40 00 00 00 00 40 00 00 20 00 00 00 02 00 00  .@....@.. ......
000000C0  04 00 00 00 00 00 00 00 04 00 00 00 00 00 00 00  ................
000000D0  00 80 00 00 00 02 00 00 00 00 00 00 03 00 40 85  .€...........@...
000000E0  00 00 10 00 00 10 00 00 00 00 10 00 00 10 00 00  ................
000000F0  00 00 00 00 10 00 00 00                          ........
```

```
/* PE header Windows NT-specific fields*/
                    00 00 00 00 00 00 00 00  ................
00000100  6C 27 00 00 4F 00 00 00 00 40 00 00 20 05 00 00  l'..O....@.. ...
00000110  00 00 00 00 00 00 00 00 00 00 00 00 00 00 00 00  ................
00000120  00 60 00 00 0C 00 00 00 EC 26 00 00 1C 00 00 00  .`......ì&......
00000130  00 00 00 00 00 00 00 00 00 00 00 00 00 00 00 00  ................
00000140  00 00 00 00 00 00 00 00 00 00 00 00 00 00 00 00  ................
00000150  00 00 00 00 00 00 00 00 00 20 00 00 08 00 00 00  ......... ......
00000160  00 00 00 00 00 00 00 00 08 20 00 00 48 00 00 00  ......... ..H...
00000170  00 00 00 00 00 00 00 00                          ........
```

```
/*Section Header*/
                                  2E 74 65 78 74 00 00 00   ........text...
00000180  C4 07 00 00 00 20 00 00 00 08 00 00 00 02 00 00   Ä.... .........
00000190  00 00 00 00 00 00 00 00 00 00 00 00 20 00 00 60   ............ ..`
000001A0  2E 72 73 72 63 00 00 00 20 05 00 00 00 40 00 00   .rsrc... ....@..
000001B0  00 06 00 00 00 0A 00 00 00 00 00 00 00 00 00 00   ................
000001C0  00 00 00 00 40 00 00 40 2E 72 65 6C 6F 63 00 00   ....@..@.reloc..
000001D0  0C 00 00 00 00 60 00 00 00 02 00 00 00 10 00 00   .....`..........
000001E0  00 00 00 00 00 00 00 00 00 00 00 00 40 00 00 42   ............@..B


000001F0  00 00 00 00 00 00 00 00 00 00 00 00 00 00 00 00   ................


/*.text section*/

00000200  A0 27 00 00 00 00 00 00                            '......
                                  48 00 00 00 02 00 05 00         H.......
00000210  8C 20 00 00 60 06 00 00 03 00 00 00 01 00 00 06   Œ ..`..........
00000220  00 00 00 00 00 00 00 00 00 00 00 00 00 00 00 00   ................
00000230  00 00 00 00 00 00 00 00 00 00 00 00 00 00 00 00   ................
00000240  00 00 00 00 00 00 00 00 00 00 00 00 00 00 00 00   ................
00000250  13 30 01 00 0F 00 00 00 01 00 00 11 00 73 04 00   .0...........s..
00000260  00 06 0A 06 6F 03 00 00 06 00 2A 1E 02 28 11 00   ....o.....*..(..
00000270  00 0A 2A 36 00 72 01 00 00 70 28 12 00 00 0A 00   ..*6.r...p(.....
00000280  2A 1E 02 28 11 00 00 0A 2A 00 00 00 42 53 4A 42   *..(....*...BSJB
00000290  01 00 01 00 00 00 00 00 0C 00 00 00 76 34 2E 30   ............v4.0
000002A0  2E 33 30 33 31 39 00 00 00 00 05 00               .30319......
                                  6C 00 00 00                 l...
000002B0  14 02 00 00 23 7E 00 00 80 02 00 00 8C 02 00 00   ....#~..€...Œ...
000002C0  23 53 74 72 69 6E 67 73 00 00 00 00 0C 05 00 00   #Strings........
000002D0  18 00 00 00 23 55 53 00 24 05 00 00 10 00 00 00   ....#US.$.......
000002E0  23 47 55 49 44 00 00 00 34 05 00 00 2C 01 00 00   #GUID...4...,...
000002F0  23 42 6C 6F 62 00 00 00                            #Blob..........
                                  00 00 00 00 02 00 00 01   #Blob..........
00000300  47 15 02 00 09 00 00 00 00 FA 25 33 00 16 00 00   G........ú%3....

00000310  01 00 00 00 13 00 00 00 03 00 00 00 04 00 00 00   ................
00000320  01 00 00 00 12 00 00 00 0E 00 00 00 01 00 00 00   ................
00000330  01 00 00 00 01 00 00 00                            ................
                                  00 00 0A 00 01 00 00 00    ................
00000340  00 00 06 00 37 00 30 00 06 00 6E 00 54 00 06 00   ....7.0...n.T...
00000350  99 00 87 00 06 00 B0 00 87 00 06 00 CD 00 87 00   ™.‡...°.‡...Í.‡.
00000360  06 00 EC 00 87 00 06 00 05 01 87 00 06 00 1E 01   ..ì.‡.....‡.....
00000370  87 00 06 00 39 01 87 00 06 00 54 01 87 00 06 00   ‡...9.‡...T.‡...
00000380  8C 01 6D 01 06 00 A0 01 6D 01 06 00 AE 01 87 00   Œ.m... .m...®.‡.
00000390  06 00 C7 01 87 00 06 00 F7 01 E4 01 3F 00 0B 02   ..Ç.‡...÷.ä.?...
000003A0  00 00 06 00 3A 02 1A 02 06 00 5A 02 1A 02 06 00   ....:.....Z.....
000003B0  78 02 30 00 00 00 00 00 01 00 00 00 00 00 01 00   x.0.............
000003C0  01 00 00 00 10 00 14 00 1C 00 05 00 01 00 01 00   ................
000003D0  01 00 10 00 22 00 1C 00 05 00 01 00 03 00 50 20   ...."..........P
000003E0  00 00 00 00 91 00 3E 00 0A 00 01 00 6B 20 00 00   ....'.>.....k ..
```

```
000003F0   00 00 86 18 43 00 10 00 02 00 73 20 00 00 00 00   ..†.C.....s ....
00000400   86 00 49 00 10 00 02 00 81 20 00 00 00 00 86 18   †.I...... ....†.
00000410   43 00 10 00 02 00 00 00 01 00 4F 00 11 00 43 00   C.........O...C.
00000420   14 00 19 00 43 00 14 00 21 00 43 00 14 00 29 00   ....C...!.C...).
00000430   43 00 14 00 31 00 43 00 14 00 39 00 43 00 14 00   C...1.C...9.C...
00000440   41 00 43 00 14 00 49 00 43 00 14 00 51 00 43 00   A.C...I.C...Q.C.
00000450   14 00 59 00 43 00 19 00 61 00 43 00 14 00 69 00   ..Y.C...a.C...i.
00000460   43 00 14 00 71 00 43 00 14 00 79 00 43 00 1E 00   C...q.C...y.C...
00000470   89 00 43 00 24 00 91 00 43 00 10 00 09 00 43 00   ‰.C.$.'.C.....C.
00000480   10 00 99 00 80 02 2E 00 2E 00 0B 00 33 00 2E 00   ..™.€.......3...
00000490   13 00 99 00 2E 00 1B 00 A4 00 2E 00 23 00 A4 00   ..™.....g...#.g.
000004A0   2E 00 2B 00 A4 00 2E 00 33 00 99 00 2E 00 3B 00   ..+.g...3.™...;.
000004B0   AA 00 2E 00 43 00 A4 00 2E 00 53 00 A4 00 2E 00   ª...C.g...S.g...
000004C0   5B 00 C2 00 2E 00 6B 00 EC 00 2E 00 73 00 F9 00   [.Â...k.ì...s.ù.
000004D0   2E 00 7B 00 02 01 2E 00 83 00 0B 01 29 00 04 80   ..{.....ƒ...)..€
000004E0   00 00 01 00 00 00 00 00 00 00 00 00 00 00 00 00   ...............
000004F0   1C 00 00 00 04 00 00 00 00 00 00 00 00 00 00 00   ...............
00000500   01 00 27 00 00 00 00 00 00 00 00 00 00            ..'.........
                                            00 3C 4D 6F      ..'.........<Mo
00000510   64 75 6C 65 3E 00 43 48 5F 30 33 2E 65 78 65 00   dule>.CH_03.exe.
00000520   50 72 6F 67 72 61 6D 00 43 48 5F 30 33 00 42 6F   Program.CH_03.Bo
00000530   6F 6B 00 6D 73 63 6F 72 6C 69 62 00 53 79 73 74   ok.mscorlib.Syst
00000540   65 6D 00 4F 62 6A 65 63 74 00 4D 61 69 6E 00 2E   em.Object.Main..
00000550   63 74 6F 72 00 50 72 69 6E 74 00 61 72 67 73 00   ctor.Print.args.
00000560   53 79 73 74 65 6D 2E 52 75 6E 74 69 6D 65 2E 56   System.Runtime.V
00000570   65 72 73 69 6F 6E 69 6E 67 00 54 61 72 67 65 74   ersioning.Target
00000580   46 72 61 6D 65 77 6F 72 6B 41 74 74 72 69 62 75   FrameworkAttribu
00000590   74 65 00 53 79 73 74 65 6D 2E 52 65 66 6C 65 63   te.System.Reflec
000005A0   74 69 6F 6E 00 41 73 73 65 6D 62 6C 79 54 69 74   tion.AssemblyTit
000005B0   6C 65 41 74 74 72 69 62 75 74 65 00 41 73 73 65   leAttribute.Asse
000005C0   6D 62 6C 79 44 65 73 63 72 69 70 74 69 6F 6E 41   mblyDescriptionA
000005D0   74 74 72 69 62 75 74 65 00 41 73 73 65 6D 62 6C   ttribute.Assembl
000005E0   79 43 6F 6E 66 69 67 75 72 61 74 69 6F 6E 41 74   yConfigurationAt
000005F0   74 72 69 62 75 74 65 00 41 73 73 65 6D 62 6C 79   tribute.Assembly
00000600   43 6F 6D 70 61 6E 79 41 74 74 72 69 62 75 74 65   CompanyAttribute
00000610   00 41 73 73 65 6D 62 6C 79 50 72 6F 64 75 63 74   .AssemblyProduct
00000620   41 74 74 72 69 62 75 74 65 00 41 73 73 65 6D 62   Attribute.Assemb
00000630   6C 79 43 6F 70 79 72 69 67 68 74 41 74 74 72 69   lyCopyrightAttri
00000640   62 75 74 65 00 41 73 73 65 6D 62 6C 79 54 72 61   bute.AssemblyTra
00000650   64 65 6D 61 72 6B 41 74 74 72 69 62 75 74 65 00   demarkAttribute.
00000660   41 73 73 65 6D 62 6C 79 43 75 6C 74 75 72 65 41   AssemblyCultureA
00000670   74 74 72 69 62 75 74 65 00 53 79 73 74 65 6D 2E   ttribute.System.
00000680   52 75 6E 74 69 6D 65 2E 49 6E 74 65 72 6F 70 53   Runtime.InteropS
00000690   65 72 76 69 63 65 73 00 43 6F 6D 56 69 73 69 62   ervices.ComVisib
000006A0   6C 65 41 74 74 72 69 62 75 74 65 00 47 75 69 64   leAttribute.Guid
000006B0   41 74 74 72 69 62 75 74 65 00 41 73 73 65 6D 62   Attribute.Assemb
000006C0   6C 79 56 65 72 73 69 6F 6E 41 74 74 72 69 62 75   lyVersionAttribu
000006D0   74 65 00 41 73 73 65 6D 62 6C 79 46 69 6C 65 56   te.AssemblyFileV
000006E0   65 72 73 69 6F 6E 41 74 74 72 69 62 75 74 65 00   ersionAttribute.
000006F0   53 79 73 74 65 6D 2E 44 69 61 67 6E 6F 73 74 69   System.Diagnosti
00000700   63 73 00 44 65 62 75 67 67 61 62 6C 65 41 74 74   cs.DebuggableAtt
```

```
00000710  72 69 62 75 74 65 00 44 65 62 75 67 67 69 6E 67   ribute.Debugging
00000720  4D 6F 64 65 73 00 53 79 73 74 65 6D 2E 52 75 6E   Modes.System.Run
00000730  74 69 6D 65 2E 43 6F 6D 70 69 6C 65 72 53 65 72   time.CompilerSer
00000740  76 69 63 65 73 00 43 6F 6D 70 69 6C 61 74 69 6F   vices.Compilatio
00000750  6E 52 65 6C 61 78 61 74 69 6F 6E 73 41 74 74 72   nRelaxationsAttr
00000760  69 62 75 74 65 00 52 75 6E 74 69 6D 65 43 6F 6D   ibute.RuntimeCom
00000770  70 61 74 69 62 69 6C 69 74 79 41 74 74 72 69 62   patibilityAttrib
00000780  75 74 65 00 43 6F 6E 73 6F 6C 65 00 57 72 69 74   ute.Console.Writ
00000790  65 4C 69 6E 65 00 00 00 00 13 42 00 6C 00 75 00   eLine.....B.l.u.

000007A0  65 00 20 00 53 00 6B 00 79 00 2E 00 00 00 00 00   e. .S.k.y.......
000007B0  EE 52 B2 1D 54 A1 C2 4E 84 22 C3 B6 D1 C0 A1 24   îR2.T¡ÂN„"Ã¶ÑÀ¡$
000007C0  00 08 B7 7A 5C 56 19 34 E0 89 05 00 01 01 1D 0E   ..·z\V.4à‰......
000007D0  03 20 00 01 04 20 01 01 0E 04 20 01 01 02 05 20   . ... .... .... 
000007E0  01 01 11 41 04 20 01 01 08 04 07 01 12 0C 04 00   ...A. .........
000007F0  01 01 0E 65 01 00 29 2E 4E 45 54 46 72 61 6D 65   ...e..).NETFrame
00000800  77 6F 72 6B 2C 56 65 72 73 69 6F 6E 3D 76 34 2E   work,Version=v4.
00000810  30 2C 50 72 6F 66 69 6C 65 3D 43 6C 69 65 6E 74   0,Profile=Client
00000820  01 00 54 0E 14 46 72 61 6D 65 77 6F 72 6B 44 69   ..T..FrameworkDi
00000830  73 70 6C 61 79 4E 61 6D 65 1F 2E 4E 45 54 20 46   splayName..NET F
00000840  72 61 6D 65 77 6F 72 6B 20 34 20 43 6C 69 65 6E   ramework 4 Clien
00000850  74 20 50 72 6F 66 69 6C 65 0A 01 00 05 43 48 5F   t Profile....CH_
00000860  30 33 00 00 05 01 00 00 00 00 17 01 00 12 43 6F   03............Co
00000870  70 79 72 69 67 68 74 20 C2 A9 20 20 32 30 31 34   pyright Â©  2014
00000880  00 00 29 01 00 24 65 36 36 61 61 32 64 31 2D 36   ..)..$e66aa2d1-6
00000890  36 66 65 2D 34 64 62 62 2D 38 36 31 63 2D 65 35   6fe-4dbb-861c-e5
000008A0  38 30 30 65 38 33 32 36 66 61 00 00 0C 01 00 07   800e8326fa......
000008B0  31 2E 30 2E 30 2E 30 00 00 08 01 00 07 01 00 00   1.0.0.0........
000008C0  00 00 08 01 00 08 00 00 00 00 00 1E 01 00 01 00   ...............
000008D0  54 02 16 57 72 61 70 4E 6F 6E 45 78 63 65 70 74   T..WrapNonExcept
000008E0  69 6F 6E 54 68 72 6F 77 73 01 00 00 00 00 00 00   ionThrows.......
000008F0  A5 0D 2D 53 00 00 00 00 02 00 00 00 63 00 00 00   ¥.-S........c...
00000900  08 27 00 00 08 09 00 00 52 53 44 53 D2 4D C2 AC   .'......RSDSÒMÂ¬
00000910  C0 A3 5A 44 A8 61 E6 CE F4 64 91 02 01 00 00 00   À£ZD¨æÎôd'.....
00000920  4A 3A 5C 42 6F 6F 6B 5C 43 23 20 44 65 63 6F 6E   J:\Book\C# Decon
00000930  73 74 72 75 63 74 65 64 5C 53 6F 75 72 63 65 43   structed\SourceC
00000940  6F 64 65 5C 43 68 61 70 74 65 72 73 5C 43 48 5F   ode\Chapters\CH_
00000950  30 33 5C 6F 62 6A 5C 78 38 36 5C 44 65 62 75 67   03\obj\x86\Debug
00000960  5C 43 48 5F 30 33 2E 70 64 62 00 00 94 27 00 00   \CH_03.pdb..”'..
00000970  00 00 00 00 00 00 00 00 AE 27 00 00 00 20 00 00   ........®'... ..
00000980  00 00 00 00 00 00 00 00 00 00 00 00 00 00 00 00   ................
00000990  00 00 00 00 A0 27 00 00 00 00 00 00 00 00 00 00   .... '..........
000009A0  00 00 5F 43 6F 72 45 78 65 4D 61 69 6E 00 6D 73   .._CorExeMain.ms
000009B0  63 6F 72 65 65 2E 64 6C 6C 00 00 00 00 00 FF 25   coree.dll.....ÿ%
000009C0  00 20 40 00 00 00 00 00 00 00 00 00 00 00 00 00   . @.............
000009D0  00 00 00 00 00 00 00 00 00 00 00 00 00 00 00 00   ................
000009E0  00 00 00 00 00 00 00 00 00 00 00 00 00 00 00 00   ................
000009F0  00 00 00 00 00 00 00 00 00 00 00 00 00 00 00 00   ................
/* end of .text Section*/
```

/* begin of .rsrc Section*/

```
00000A00   00 00 00 00 00 00 00 00 00 00 00 00 00 00 02 00   ..............
00000A10   10 00 00 00 20 00 00 80 18 00 00 00 38 00 00 80   .... ..€....8..€
00000A20   00 00 00 00 00 00 00 00 00 00 00 00 00 00 01 00   ..............
00000A30   01 00 00 00 50 00 00 80 00 00 00 00 00 00 00 00   ....P..€........
00000A40   00 00 00 00 00 00 01 00 01 00 00 00 68 00 00 80   ............h..€
00000A50   00 00 00 00 00 00 00 00 00 00 00 00 00 00 01 00   ..............
00000A60   00 00 00 00 80 00 00 00 00 00 00 00 00 00 00 00   ....€.........
00000A70   00 00 00 00 00 00 01 00 00 00 00 00 90 00 00 00   ..............
00000A80   A0 40 00 00 90 02 00 00 00 00 00 00 00 00 00 00   @............
00000A90   30 43 00 00 EA 01 00 00 00 00 00 00 00 00 00 00   0C..ê..........
00000AA0   90 02 34 00 00 00 56 00 53 00 5F 00 56 00 45 00   ..4...V.S._.V.E.
00000AB0   52 00 53 00 49 00 4F 00 4E 00 5F 00 49 00 4E 00   R.S.I.O.N._.I.N.
00000AC0   46 00 4F 00 00 00 00 00 BD 04 EF FE 00 00 01 00   F.O.....½.ïþ....
00000AD0   00 00 01 00 00 00 00 00 00 00 01 00 00 00 00 00   ..............
00000AE0   3F 00 00 00 00 00 00 00 04 00 00 00 01 00 00 00   ?.............
00000AF0   00 00 00 00 00 00 00 00 00 00 00 00 44 00 00 00   ............D...
00000B00   01 00 56 00 61 00 72 00 46 00 69 00 6C 00 65 00   ..V.a.r.F.i.l.e.
00000B10   49 00 6E 00 66 00 6F 00 00 00 00 00 24 00 04 00   I.n.f.o.....$...
00000B20   00 00 54 00 72 00 61 00 6E 00 73 00 6C 00 61 00   ..T.r.a.n.s.l.a.
00000B30   74 00 69 00 6F 00 6E 00 00 00 00 00 00 00 B0 04   t.i.o.n.......°.
00000B40   F0 01 00 00 01 00 53 00 74 00 72 00 69 00 6E 00   ð.....S.t.r.i.n.
00000B50   67 00 46 00 69 00 6C 00 65 00 49 00 6E 00 66 00   g.F.i.l.e.I.n.f.
00000B60   6F 00 00 00 CC 01 00 00 01 00 30 00 30 00 30 00   o...Ì.....0.0.0.
00000B70   30 00 30 00 34 00 62 00 30 00 00 00 34 00 06 00   0.0.4.b.0...4...
00000B80   01 00 46 00 69 00 6C 00 65 00 44 00 65 00 73 00   ..F.i.l.e.D.e.s.
00000B90   63 00 72 00 69 00 70 00 74 00 69 00 6F 00 6E 00   c.r.i.p.t.i.o.n.
00000BA0   00 00 00 00 43 00 48 00 5F 00 30 00 33 00 00 00   ....C.H._.0.3...
00000BB0   30 00 08 00 01 00 46 00 69 00 6C 00 65 00 56 00   0.....F.i.l.e.V.
00000BC0   65 00 72 00 73 00 69 00 6F 00 6E 00 00 00 00 00   e.r.s.i.o.n.....
00000BD0   31 00 2E 00 30 00 2E 00 30 00 2E 00 30 00 00 00   1...0...0...0...
00000BE0   34 00 0A 00 01 00 49 00 6E 00 74 00 65 00 72 00   4.....I.n.t.e.r.
00000BF0   6E 00 61 00 6C 00 4E 00 61 00 6D 00 65 00 00 00   n.a.l.N.a.m.e...
00000C00   43 00 48 00 5F 00 30 00 33 00 2E 00 65 00 78 00   C.H._.0.3...e.x.
00000C10   65 00 00 00 48 00 12 00 01 00 4C 00 65 00 67 00   e...H.....L.e.g.
00000C20   61 00 6C 00 43 00 6F 00 70 00 79 00 72 00 69 00   a.l.C.o.p.y.r.i.
00000C30   67 00 68 00 74 00 00 00 43 00 6F 00 70 00 79 00   g.h.t...C.o.p.y.
00000C40   72 00 69 00 67 00 68 00 74 00 20 00 A9 00 20 00   r.i.g.h.t. .©. .
00000C50   20 00 32 00 30 00 31 00 34 00 00 00 3C 00 0A 00    .2.0.1.4...<...
00000C60   01 00 4F 00 72 00 69 00 67 00 69 00 6E 00 61 00   ..O.r.i.g.i.n.a.
00000C70   6C 00 46 00 69 00 6C 00 65 00 6E 00 61 00 6D 00   l.F.i.l.e.n.a.m.
00000C80   65 00 00 00 43 00 48 00 5F 00 30 00 33 00 2E 00   e...C.H._.0.3...
00000C90   65 00 78 00 65 00 00 00 2C 00 06 00 01 00 50 00   e.x.e...,.....P.
00000CA0   72 00 6F 00 64 00 75 00 63 00 74 00 4E 00 61 00   r.o.d.u.c.t.N.a.
00000CB0   6D 00 65 00 00 00 00 00 43 00 48 00 5F 00 30 00   m.e.....C.H._.0.
00000CC0   33 00 00 00 34 00 08 00 01 00 50 00 72 00 6F 00   3...4.....P.r.o.
00000CD0   64 00 75 00 63 00 74 00 56 00 65 00 72 00 73 00   d.u.c.t.V.e.r.s.
00000CE0   69 00 6F 00 6E 00 00 00 31 00 2E 00 30 00 2E 00   i.o.n...1...0...
00000CF0   30 00 2E 00 30 00 00 00 38 00 08 00 01 00 41 00   0...0...8.....A.
00000D00   73 00 73 00 65 00 6D 00 62 00 6C 00 79 00 20 00   s.s.e.m.b.l.y. .
```

```
00000D10    56 00 65 00 72 00 73 00 69 00 6F 00 6E 00 00 00    V.e.r.s.i.o.n...
00000D20    31 00 2E 00 30 00 2E 00 30 00 2E 00 30 00 00 00    1...0...0...0...
00000D30    EF BB BF 3C 3F 78 6D 6C 20 76 65 72 73 69 6F 6E    ï»¿<?xml version
00000D40    3D 22 31 2E 30 22 20 65 6E 63 6F 64 69 6E 67 3D    ="1.0" encoding=
00000D50    22 55 54 46 2D 38 22 20 73 74 61 6E 64 61 6C 6F    "UTF-8" standalo
00000D60    6E 65 3D 22 79 65 73 22 3F 3E 0D 0A 3C 61 73 73    ne="yes"?>..<ass
00000D70    65 6D 62 6C 79 20 78 6D 6C 6E 73 3D 22 75 72 6E    embly xmlns="urn
00000D80    3A 73 63 68 65 6D 61 73 2D 6D 69 63 72 6F 73 6F    :schemas-microso
00000D90    66 74 2D 63 6F 6D 3A 61 73 6D 2E 76 31 22 20 6D    ft-com:asm.v1" m
00000DA0    61 6E 69 66 65 73 74 56 65 72 73 69 6F 6E 3D 22    anifestVersion="
00000DB0    31 2E 30 22 3E 0D 0A 20 20 3C 61 73 73 65 6D 62    1.0">..  <assemb
00000DC0    6C 79 49 64 65 6E 74 69 74 79 20 76 65 72 73 69    lyIdentity versi
00000DD0    6F 6E 3D 22 31 2E 30 2E 30 2E 30 22 20 6E 61 6D    on="1.0.0.0" nam
00000DE0    65 3D 22 4D 79 41 70 70 6C 69 63 61 74 69 6F 6E    e="MyApplication
00000DF0    2E 61 70 70 22 2F 3E 0D 0A 20 20 3C 74 72 75 73    .app"/>..  <trus
00000E00    74 49 6E 66 6F 20 78 6D 6C 6E 73 3D 22 75 72 6E    tInfo xmlns="urn
00000E10    3A 73 63 68 65 6D 61 73 2D 6D 69 63 72 6F 73 6F    :schemas-microso
00000E20    66 74 2D 63 6F 6D 3A 61 73 6D 2E 76 32 22 3E 0D    ft-com:asm.v2">.
00000E30    0A 20 20 20 20 3C 73 65 63 75 72 69 74 79 3E 0D    .    <security>.
00000E40    0A 20 20 20 20 20 20 3C 72 65 71 75 65 73 74 65    .      <requeste
00000E50    64 50 72 69 76 69 6C 65 67 65 73 20 78 6D 6C 6E    dPrivileges xmln
00000E60    73 3D 22 75 72 6E 3A 73 63 68 65 6D 61 73 2D 6D    s="urn:schemas-m
00000E70    69 63 72 6F 73 6F 66 74 2D 63 6F 6D 3A 61 73 6D    icrosoft-com:asm
00000E80    2E 76 33 22 3E 0D 0A 20 20 20 20 20 20 20 20 3C    .v3">..        <
00000E90    72 65 71 75 65 73 74 65 64 45 78 65 63 75 74 69    requestedExecuti
00000EA0    6F 6E 4C 65 76 65 6C 20 6C 65 76 65 6C 3D 22 61    onLevel level="a
00000EB0    73 49 6E 76 6F 6B 65 72 22 20 75 69 41 63 63 65    sInvoker" uiAcce
00000EC0    73 73 3D 22 66 61 6C 73 65 22 2F 3E 0D 0A 20 20    ss="false"/>..  
00000ED0    20 20 20 20 3C 2F 72 65 71 75 65 73 74 65 64 50        </requestedP
00000EE0    72 69 76 69 6C 65 67 65 73 3E 0D 0A 20 20 20 20    rivileges>..    
00000EF0    3C 2F 73 65 63 75 72 69 74 79 3E 0D 0A 20 20 3C    </security>..  <
00000F00    2F 74 72 75 73 74 49 6E 66 6F 3E 0D 0A 3C 2F 61    /trustInfo>..</a
00000F10    73 73 65 6D 62 6C 79 3E 0D 0A 00 00 00 00 00 00    ssembly>........
00000F20    00 00 00 00 00 00 00 00 00 00 00 00 00 00 00 00    ................
00000F30    00 00 00 00 00 00 00 00 00 00 00 00 00 00 00 00    ................
00000F40    00 00 00 00 00 00 00 00 00 00 00 00 00 00 00 00    ................
00000F50    00 00 00 00 00 00 00 00 00 00 00 00 00 00 00 00    ................
00000F60    00 00 00 00 00 00 00 00 00 00 00 00 00 00 00 00    ................
00000F70    00 00 00 00 00 00 00 00 00 00 00 00 00 00 00 00    ................
00000F80    00 00 00 00 00 00 00 00 00 00 00 00 00 00 00 00    ................
00000F90    00 00 00 00 00 00 00 00 00 00 00 00 00 00 00 00    ................
00000FA0    00 00 00 00 00 00 00 00 00 00 00 00 00 00 00 00    ................
00000FB0    00 00 00 00 00 00 00 00 00 00 00 00 00 00 00 00    ................
00000FC0    00 00 00 00 00 00 00 00 00 00 00 00 00 00 00 00    ................
00000FD0    00 00 00 00 00 00 00 00 00 00 00 00 00 00 00 00    ................
00000FE0    00 00 00 00 00 00 00 00 00 00 00 00 00 00 00 00    ................
00000FF0    00 00 00 00 00 00 00 00 00 00 00 00 00 00 00 00    ................

00001000    00 20 00 00 0C 00 00 00 C0 37 00 00 00 00 00 00    . ......À7......
00001010    00 00 00 00 00 00 00 00 00 00 00 00 00 00 00 00    ................
00001020    00 00 00 00 00 00 00 00 00 00 00 00 00 00 00 00    ................
```

```
00001030  00 00 00 00 00 00 00 00 00 00 00 00 00 00 00 00   ................
00001040  00 00 00 00 00 00 00 00 00 00 00 00 00 00 00 00   ................
00001050  00 00 00 00 00 00 00 00 00 00 00 00 00 00 00 00   ................
00001060  00 00 00 00 00 00 00 00 00 00 00 00 00 00 00 00   ................
00001070  00 00 00 00 00 00 00 00 00 00 00 00 00 00 00 00   ................
00001080  00 00 00 00 00 00 00 00 00 00 00 00 00 00 00 00   ................
00001090  00 00 00 00 00 00 00 00 00 00 00 00 00 00 00 00   ................
000010A0  00 00 00 00 00 00 00 00 00 00 00 00 00 00 00 00   ................
000010B0  00 00 00 00 00 00 00 00 00 00 00 00 00 00 00 00   ................
000010C0  00 00 00 00 00 00 00 00 00 00 00 00 00 00 00 00   ................
000010D0  00 00 00 00 00 00 00 00 00 00 00 00 00 00 00 00   ................
000010E0  00 00 00 00 00 00 00 00 00 00 00 00 00 00 00 00   ................
000010F0  00 00 00 00 00 00 00 00 00 00 00 00 00 00 00 00   ................
00001100  00 00 00 00 00 00 00 00 00 00 00 00 00 00 00 00   ................
00001110  00 00 00 00 00 00 00 00 00 00 00 00 00 00 00 00   ................
00001120  00 00 00 00 00 00 00 00 00 00 00 00 00 00 00 00   ................
00001130  00 00 00 00 00 00 00 00 00 00 00 00 00 00 00 00   ................
00001140  00 00 00 00 00 00 00 00 00 00 00 00 00 00 00 00   ................
00001150  00 00 00 00 00 00 00 00 00 00 00 00 00 00 00 00   ................
00001160  00 00 00 00 00 00 00 00 00 00 00 00 00 00 00 00   ................
00001170  00 00 00 00 00 00 00 00 00 00 00 00 00 00 00 00   ................
00001180  00 00 00 00 00 00 00 00 00 00 00 00 00 00 00 00   ................
00001190  00 00 00 00 00 00 00 00 00 00 00 00 00 00 00 00   ................
000011A0  00 00 00 00 00 00 00 00 00 00 00 00 00 00 00 00   ................
000011B0  00 00 00 00 00 00 00 00 00 00 00 00 00 00 00 00   ................
000011C0  00 00 00 00 00 00 00 00 00 00 00 00 00 00 00 00   ................
000011D0  00 00 00 00 00 00 00 00 00 00 00 00 00 00 00 00   ................
000011E0  00 00 00 00 00 00 00 00 00 00 00 00 00 00 00 00   ................
000011F0  00 00 00 00 00 00 00 00 00 00 00 00 00 00 00 00   ................
```

HXD: HEX EDITOR

In this chapter the HxD tool is used to open the assembly file in hexadecimal format. This tool can be downloaded from the mh-nexus web site: (http://mh-nexus.de/en).

Analysis of the Assembly

Within the assembly the MS-DOS header is followed by the PE signature and then the PE file header and the PE optional header. The PE optional header has its own subheaders, such as standard fields, NT-specific fields, and data directories. Next is the section header. The section header contains information on the sections, such as .text, .rsrc, and .reloc.

The .text section is important, as it provides the CLI header, metadata, IL code, and other information, which you will explore later in the chapter. Before we move into that discussion, let's take a look at how each of the sections has been defined and referenced by the assembly's section header Figure 3-3 illustrates the assembly contents.

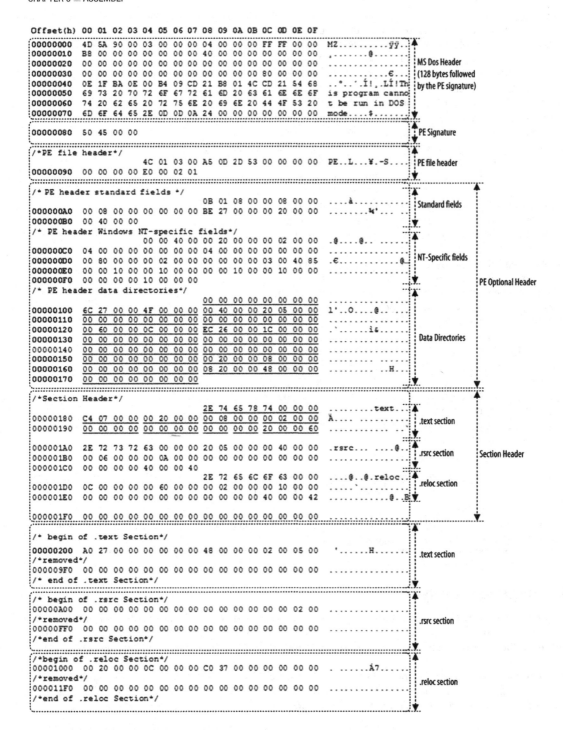

Figure 3-3. *A typical .NET assembly in hexadecimal format*

Section Header

According to Partition 2, clause 25.3 of the ECMA C# standard, section headers contain the information provided in Table 3-1.

Table 3-1. *Section Headers*

Size	Field	Description
8	Name	An 8-byte, null-padded ASCII string. There is no terminating null if the string is exactly eight characters long.
4	VirtualSize	Total size of the section, in bytes. If this value is greater than SizeOfRawData, the section is zero padded.
4	VirtualAddress	For executable images this is the address of the first byte of the section when loaded into memory, relative to the image base.
4	SizeOfRawData	Size of the initialized data on disk, in bytes; will be a multiple of FileAlignment, from the PE header. If this is less than VirtualSize, the remainder of the section is zero filled. Because this field is rounded, whereas the VirtualSize field is not, it is possible for this to be greater than VirtualSize as well. When a section contains only uninitialized data, this field should be 0.
4	PointerToRawData	Offset of the section's first page in the PE file. This will be a multiple of FileAlignment, from the optional header. When a section contains only uninitialized data, this field should be 0.
4	PointerToRelocations	Relative virtual address (RVA) of the .reloc section.
4	PointerToLinenumbers	Always 0 (§24.1).
2	NumberOfRelocations	Number of relocations; set to 0 if unused.
2	NumberOfLinenumbers	Always 0 (§24.1).
4	Characteristics	Flags describing a section's characteristics.

From the PE file header contents, you can determine that there are three sections in the assembly and that each of the sections is 40 bytes long, making the section header a total of 120 bytes long. It starts where the PE optional header ends. The section header contents from the hexadecimal output from Listing 3-1 are as follows:

```
Offset(h) 00 01 02 03 04 05 06 07 08 09 0A 0B 0C 0D 0E 0F
/*Section Header*/
                              2E 74 65 78 74 00 00 00          .text...
00000180  C4 07 00 00 00 20 00 00 00 08 00 00 00 02 00 00  Ä.... .........
00000190  00 00 00 00 00 00 00 00 00 00 00 00 20 00 00 60  ............ ..`

000001A0  2E 72 73 72 63 00 00 00 20 05 00 00 00 40 00 00  .rsrc... ....@..
000001B0  00 06 00 00 00 0A 00 00 00 00 00 00 00 00 00 00  ...............
000001C0  00 00 00 00 40 00 00 40                          ....@..@
                              2E 72 65 6C 6F 63 00 00          .reloc..
000001D0  0C 00 00 00 00 60 00 00 00 02 00 00 00 10 00 00  .....`.........
000001E0  00 00 00 00 00 00 00 00 00 00 00 00 40 00 00 42  ............@..B

000001F0  00 00 00 00 00 00 00 00 00 00 00 00 00 00 00 00  ...............
```

Using the hexadecimal output, let's take a closer look at the first 40 bytes to get a better understanding of the first section:

```
Offset(h) 00 01 02 03 04 05 06 07 08 09 0A 0B 0C 0D 0E 0F
/*Section Header*/
                        2E 74 65 78 74 00 00 00              .text...
00000180  C4 07 00 00 00 20 00 00 00 08 00 00 00 02 00 00  Ä.... .........
00000190  00 00 00 00 00 00 00 00 00 00 00 00 20 00 00 60  ............ ..`
```

According to the header specification the first 8 bytes define the name of the section, so 00 00 00 2E 74 65 78 74 refers to the .text section. So, this is the .text section, and it has 00 00 07 C4 as virtual size, 00 00 20 00 as virtual address, 00 00 08 00 as raw size, and 00 00 20 00 as raw address. The size of the .text section is 7C4 bytes, starting from the offset 200. Based on this the end location of the .text section can be calculated as 200 + 7C4 = 9C4. But, the actual size of the .text section is defined as 800 bytes by the compiler. According to the specification, the remaining 3C bytes (800 – 7C4 = 3C) needs to pad with 0 (marked with underline), increasing the total length of the .text section to 9C4 + 3C = A00 (which is actually 9FF). Thus, the total .text section will be as shown:

```
Offset(h) 00 01 02 03 04 05 06 07 08 09 0A 0B 0C 0D 0E 0F
/* begin of .text Section*/
00000200  A0 27 00 00 00 00 00 00 48 00 00 00 02 00 05 00  '......H.......
/*removed*/
000009A0  00 00 5F 43 6F 72 45 78 65 4D 61 69 6E 00 6D 73  .._CorExeMain.ms
000009B0  63 6F 72 65 65 2E 64 6C 6C 00 00 00 00 00 FF 25  coree.dll.....ÿ%
000009C0  00 20 40 00 00 00 00 00 00 00 00 00 00 00 00 00  . @............
000009D0  00 00 00 00 00 00 00 00 00 00 00 00 00 00 00 00  ................
000009E0  00 00 00 00 00 00 00 00 00 00 00 00 00 00 00 00  ................
000009F0  00 00 00 00 00 00 00 00 00 00 00 00 00 00 00 00  ................
/* end of .text Section*/
```

Now, let's take a look at the next 40 bytes to understand the next section header.:

```
.rsrc section:
000001A0  2E 72 73 72 63 00 00 00 20 05 00 00 00 40 00 00  .rsrc... ....@..
000001B0  00 06 00 00 00 0A 00 00 00 00 00 00 00 00 00 00  ................
000001C0  00 00 00 00 40 00 00 40                          
```

According to the header specification the first 8 bytes define the name, so 00 00 00 2E 72 73 72 63 refers to .rsrc. Hence, this is the .rsrc section, and it has 00 00 05 20 as virtual size, 00 00 40 00 as virtual address, 00 00 06 00 as raw size, and 00 00 A0 00 as raw address. The size of the .rsrc section is 520 bytes, starting from the offset A00. Based on this, the end location of the .rsrc section will be A00 + 520 = F20. But, the actual size of the .rsrc section is defined as 600 by the compiler. According to the specification, 600 – 520 = E0 needs to pad the end of the .rsrc section with 0 (marked with underline), up to F20 + E0 = 1000 (which is actually FFF). Therefore, the total .rsrc section will be as follows:

```
Offset(h) 00 01 02 03 04 05 06 07 08 09 0A 0B 0C 0D 0E 0F
/* begin of .rsrc Section*/
00000A00  00 00 00 00 00 00 00 00 00 00 00 00 00 00 02 00  ...............
/*removed*/
00000F00  2F 74 72 75 73 74 49 6E 66 6F 3E 0D 0A 3C 2F 61  /trustInfo>..</a
00000F10  73 73 65 6D 62 6C 79 3E 0D 0A 00 00 00 00 00 00  ssembly>........
00000F20  00 00 00 00 00 00 00 00 00 00 00 00 00 00 00 00  ................
00000F30  00 00 00 00 00 00 00 00 00 00 00 00 00 00 00 00  ................
```

```
00000F40  00 00 00 00 00 00 00 00 00 00 00 00 00 00 00 00   ...............
00000F50  00 00 00 00 00 00 00 00 00 00 00 00 00 00 00 00   ...............
00000F60  00 00 00 00 00 00 00 00 00 00 00 00 00 00 00 00   ...............
00000F70  00 00 00 00 00 00 00 00 00 00 00 00 00 00 00 00   ...............
00000F80  00 00 00 00 00 00 00 00 00 00 00 00 00 00 00 00   ...............
00000F90  00 00 00 00 00 00 00 00 00 00 00 00 00 00 00 00   ...............
00000FA0  00 00 00 00 00 00 00 00 00 00 00 00 00 00 00 00   ...............
00000FB0  00 00 00 00 00 00 00 00 00 00 00 00 00 00 00 00   ...............
00000FC0  00 00 00 00 00 00 00 00 00 00 00 00 00 00 00 00   ...............
00000FD0  00 00 00 00 00 00 00 00 00 00 00 00 00 00 00 00   ...............
00000FE0  00 00 00 00 00 00 00 00 00 00 00 00 00 00 00 00   ...............
00000FF0  00 00 00 00 00 00 00 00 00 00 00 00 00 00 00 00   ...............
00000FF0  00 00 00 00 00 00 00 00 00 00 00 00 00 00 00 00   ...............
/*end of .rsrc Section*/
```

The same technique can be applied to extract other section information. In the next section, you will examine how the .text section has been defined in the assembly.

.text Section

According to Partition 2, clause 24.2.6 of the ECMA C# standard, the specification of the #~ stream is as shown in Table 3-2.

Table 3-2. *Section Header*

Size	Field	Description
4	Reserved	Reserved; always 0.
1	MajorVersion	Major version of table schemata; will be 2.
1	MinorVersion	Minor version of table schemata; will be 0.
1	HeapSizes	Bit vector for heap sizes.
1	Reserved	Reserved; always 1.
8	Valid	Bit vector of present tables; let n be the number of bits that are 1.
8	Sorted	Bit vector of sorted tables.
4*n	Rows	Array of n 4-byte unsigned integers, indicating the number of rows for each present table.
	Tables	Sequence of physical tables.

Figure 3-4 illustrates the .text section of an assembly.

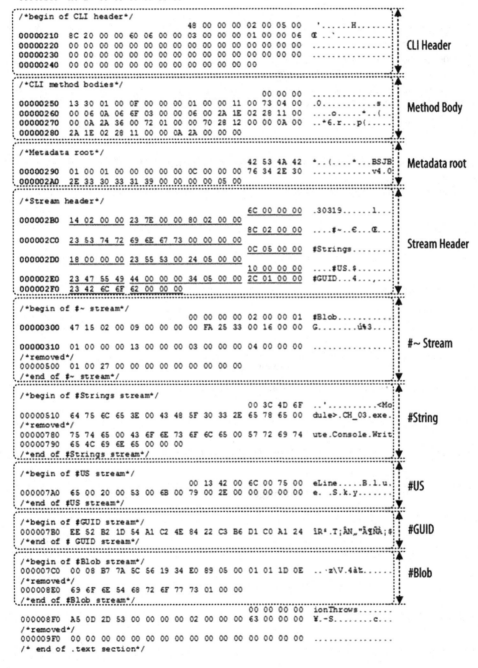

Figure 3-4. *.text section of an assenbly*

Table 3-3 shows the specification of the stream header.

Table 3-3. *Stream Header*

Size	Field	Description
4	Offset	Memory offset to the start of this stream from the start of the metadata root.
4	Size	Size of this stream, in bytes; will be a multiple of four.
	Name	Name of the stream as null-terminated, variable-length array of ASCII characters, padded to the next 4-byte boundary with \0 characters. The name is limited to 32 characters.

The `.text` section of the assembly defines the stream headers used in the assembly. The stream header data is as follows:

```
Offset(h) 00 01 02 03 04 05 06 07 08 09 0A 0B 0C 0D 0E 0F
                                          6C 00 00 00               .l...
000002B0  14 02 00 00 23 7E 00 00 80 02 00 00 8C 02 00 00  ....#~..€...Œ...
000002C0  23 53 74 72 69 6E 67 73 00 00 00 00 0C 05 00 00  #Strings........
000002D0  18 00 00 00 23 55 53 00 24 05 00 00 10 00 00 00  ....#US.$.......
000002E0  23 47 55 49 44 00 00 00 34 05 00 00 2C 01 00 00  #GUID...4...,...
000002F0  23 42 6C 6F 62 00 00 00                          #Blob...
                                 00 00 00 00 02 00 00 01            ........
00000300  47 15 02 00 09 00 00 00 00 FA 25 33 00 16 00 00  G........ú%3....
```

This hexadecimal output shows that the first 4 bytes, 6C 00 00 00, refer to the offset of this stream and are followed by another 4 bytes representing the size of the stream and an 8-byte string referring to its name. As per its definition, this #~ stream will start from the metadata root addition to the offset defined in the stream headers section. The #~ stream has an offset of 6C, and the metadata root starts at 28C, so the #~ stream will start at metadata root + 6C = 28C + 6C = 2F8. The total size of the stream is 00 00 02 14, making the end address of the #~ stream 2F8 + 214 = 50C.

```
Offset(h) 00 01 02 03 04 05 06 07 08 09 0A 0B 0C 0D 0E 0F

000002F0  23 42 6C 6F 62 00 00 00
/*begin of #~ stream*/
                                 00 00 00 00 02 00 00 01  #Blob..........
00000300  47 15 02 00 09 00 00 00 00 FA 25 33 00 16 00 00  G........ú%3....

00000310  01 00 00 00 13 00 00 00 03 00 00 00 04 00 00 00  ................
/*removed*/
00000500  01 00 27 00 00 00 00 00 00 00 00 00
/*end of #~ stream*/
```

The same technique can be used to extract other header information. In the following sections, you will study the different streams from the stream header data.

#~ stream

The type metadata are stored in tables. There are three kinds of metadata tables for types: definition tables, reference tables, and pointer tables.

Definition Tables

Each definition table contains information with respect to one type of element for the module (e.g., the classes, the methods of the classes). I will not detail all the possible tables, but include here the most important ones.

ModuleDef

This table has a single entry that defines the current module. This entry provides the name of the file, with its extension, but without its path.

TypeDef

This table presents one entry for each type defined in the module. Each entry offers the name of the type, the base type, flags for the type (public, internal, sealed), and indexes referencing the members of the types in the metadata tables (`MethodDef`, `FieldDef`, `PropertyDef`, `EventDef`, and so on).

MethodDef

This table has one entry for each method defined in the module. Each entry includes the name of the method; flags for the method (public, abstract, sealed, and so on); an offset allowing the method to be located in the IL code; and a reference to the signature of the method, which is contained in a binary form in a heap called the `#blob`. There is also a table for the fields (`FieldDef`), one for the properties (`PropertyDef`), one for events (`EventDef`), and so on. The definition of these tables is standard, and each is coded with an identification byte. For example, all the `MethodDef` tables in .NET modules have a table number of 6.

Reference Tables

Reference tables contain information on the elements referenced by the module. The referenced elements can be defined in other modules of the same assembly or as part of other assemblies. Following are a few commonly used reference tables.

AssemblyRef

This table has an entry for each assembly referenced in the module (i.e., each assembly that has at least one element referenced in the module). Each entry provides the four components of a strong name: name of the assembly (without path or extension), version number, culture, and public key token (may be null if one is not present).

ModuleRef

This table presents one entry for each module of the current assembly referenced in the module (i.e., each module that contains at least one element referenced in the module). Each entry offers the name of the module, with its extension.

TypeRef

This table has one entry for each type referenced in the module. Each entry includes the name of the type and a reference to where it is defined. If the type is defined in this module or another module of the same assembly, the reference indicates an entry in the `ModuleRef` table. If the type is defined in another assembly, the reference indicates an entry in the `AssemblyRef` table. If the type is encapsulated within another type, the reference points to an entry in the `TypeRef` table.

MemberRef

This table provides one entry for each member referenced in the module. A member can be, for example, a method, a field, or a property. Each entry includes the name of the member, its signature, and a reference to the TypeRef table. The definition of these tables is also standard, and each table is coded with a byte. For instance, all MemberRef tables in a .NET module are identified with the number 10.

In addition to these tables, the metadata section contains four heaps: #Strings, #Blob, #US, and #GUID.

The #Strings heap has character strings, such as the name of the methods. This means that elements of the tables, such as MethodDef or MemberRef, do not contain actual strings, but references to the elements of the #String heap.

The #Blob heap offers binary information, such as the method signatures, stored in a binary format. This means that elements from the MethodDef or MemberRef tables do not contain signatures, but references to the #Blob heap.

The #US (user string) includes character strings defined directly within the code.

The #GUID heap provides the globally unique identifier (GUID) defined and used in the program. A GUID is a 16-byte constant that is employed to name a resource. The particularity of a GUID is that it can be generated by tools such as guidgen.exe in a way almost certain to guarantee its uniqueness.

MEMORY LAYOUT

I hear a lot of questions about memory layout. When we talk about laying out the memory of an assembly, we simply mean reading the assembly contents at runtime; instantiating a CLR data structure in the CLR address space; and populating the data structure with the relevant the values, extracted from the assembly contents. The CLR will read the following contents (output from the C# program depicted in Listing 3-1) in hexadecimal and lay them out in the memory as an IL code block that you can explore, using the !dumpil SOS command via the WinDbg tool.

```
Offset(h) 00 01 02 03 04 05 06 07 08 09 0A 0B 0C 0D 0E 0F
                                          00 00 00  ...............
00000250  13 30 01 00 0F 00 00 00 01 00 00 11 00 73 04 00  .0...........s..
00000260  00 06 0A 06 6F 03 00 00 06 00 2A 1E 02 28 11 00  ....o.....*..(..
00000270  00 0A 2A 36 00 72 01 00 00 70 28 12 00 00 0A 00  ..*6.r...p(.....
00000280  2A 1E 02 28 11 00 00 0A 2A 00 00 00
```

Looking at the the hexadecimal output of this assembly, you can see that the #~ stream is defined in the .text section, which contains different metadata, such as ModuleDef, TypeDef, MethodDef, AssemblyRef, ModuleRef, and MemberRef, to define the types used in the program.

```
Offset(h) 00 01 02 03 04  05 06 07 08 09 0A 0B 0C 0D 0E 0F
                                       00 00 0A 00 01 00 00 00  ...............
00000340  00 00 06 00 37 00 30 00 06 00 6E 00 54 00 06 00  ....7.0...n.T...
00000350  99 00 87 00 06 00 B0 00 87 00 06 00 CD 00 87 00  ™.‡...°.‡...Í.‡.
00000360  06 00 EC 00 87 00 06 00 05 01 87 00 06 00 1E 01  ..ì.‡.....‡.....
00000370  87 00 06 00 39 01 87 00 06 00 54 01 87 00 06 00  ‡...9.‡...T.‡...
00000380  8C 01 6D 01 06 00 A0 01 6D 01 06 00 AE 01 87 00  Œ.m... .m...®.‡.
00000390  06 00 C7 01 87 00 06 00 F7 01 E4 01 3F 00 0B 02  ..Ç.‡...÷.ä.?...
000003A0  00 00 06 00 3A 02 1A 02 06 00 5A 02 1A 02 06 00  ....:.....Z.....
000003B0  78 02 30 00 00 00 00 00 00 01 00 00 00 00 00 01 00  x.0............
000003C0  01 00 00 00 10 00 14 00 1C 00 05 00 01 00 01 00  ...............
000003D0  01 00 10 00 22 00 1C 00 05 00 01 00 03 00 50 20  ...."........P
000003E0  00 00 00 00 91 00 3E 00 0A 00 01 00 6B 20 00 00  ....'.>....k ..
000003F0  00 00 86 18 43 00 10 00 02 00 73 20 00 00 00 00  ..†.C.....s ....
```

```
00000400   86 00 49 00 10 00 02 00 81 20 00 00 00 00 86 18   †.I...... ....†.
00000410   43 00 10 00 02 00 00 00 01 00 4F 00 11 00 43 00   C.........O...C.
00000420   14 00 19 00 43 00 14 00 21 00 43 00 14 00 29 00   ....C...!.C...).
00000430   43 00 14 00 31 00 43 00 14 00 39 00 43 00 14 00   C...1.C...9.C...
00000440   41 00 43 00 14 00 49 00 43 00 14 00 51 00 43 00   A.C...I.C...Q.C.
00000450   14 00 59 00 43 00 19 00 61 00 43 00 14 00 69 00   ..Y.C...a.C...i.
00000460   43 00 14 00 71 00 43 00 14 00 79 00 43 00 1E 00   C...q.C...y.C...
00000470   89 00 43 00 24 00 91 00 43 00 10 00 09 00 43 00   ‰.C.$.'.C.....C.
00000480   10 00 99 00 80 02 2E 00 2E 00 0B 00 33 00 2E 00   ..™.€.......3...
00000490   13 00 99 00 2E 00 1B 00 A4 00 2E 00 23 00 A4 00   ..™.....¤...#.¤.
000004A0   2E 00 2B 00 A4 00 2E 00 33 00 99 00 2E 00 3B 00   ..+.¤...3.™...;.
000004B0   AA 00 2E 00 43 00 A4 00 2E 00 53 00 A4 00 2E 00   ª...C.¤...S.¤...
000004C0   5B 00 C2 00 2E 00 6B 00 EC 00 2E 00 73 00 F9 00   [.Â...k.ì...s.ù.
000004D0   2E 00 7B 00 02 01 2E 00 83 00 0B 01 29 00 04 80   ..{.....ƒ...)..€
000004E0   00 00 01 00 00 00 00 00 00 00 00 00 00 00 00 00   ...............
000004F0   1C 00 00 00 04 00 00 00 00 00 00 00 00 00 00 00   ...............
00000500   01 00 27 00 00 00 00 00 00 00 00 00 00
```

The CLR will read this value and use it to lay out the type used in the assembly. You can easily find it, using !name2ee SOS command via WinDbg.

Assembly Loading

The CLR loads the assembly into memory and makes it ready to execute by the execution engine of the CLR. The assembly-loading process in the CLR consists of the following steps:

1. *Binding*: In this step the CLR determines the assembly to load. To establish the identity of the assembly, the CLR seeks information as the user inputs it or during dependency resolution and consults system configuration and the fusion subsystem.

2. *Probing*: Binding often relies on the fusion subsystem to perform probing in order to locate an assembly against which to bind. Probing encapsulates much of the complexity of locating assemblies on your system so that the CLR loader does not have to.

3. *Mapping*: Once the identity of the assembly is determined, the CLR reads and maps it in memory. The physical representation of the assembly is mapped in the virtual memory space.

4. *Loading*: The last step is to prepare the loaded code for execution. Before code can be executed, it must pass through the verification phase. Once the code is verified, the CLR creates the relevant data structures to start execution.

Mapping and loading are mostly implementation details that you seldom need to worry about. The following section discusses the loading and probing process further.

Inside the Bind, Map, Load Process

A number of steps take place to determine what code to load, where to load it from, and what context it will be loaded into. A conceptual overview of the process is depicted in Figure 3-5.

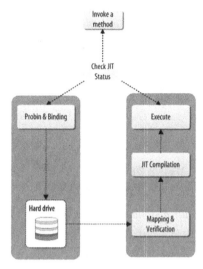

Figure 3-5. *Assembly loading*

A related part of binding is probing. Probing is the act of searching for the physical binary, based on the version and location information discovered earlier, in the loading process. Roughly speaking, these four activities can be conceptually envisioned as described in the next section.

Binding to an Assembly

The binding process accepts a variety of inputs, including either a fully or a partially qualified assembly name, a file path, or a byte[ ] block of memory. The process then uses this input to decide which bits must be loaded and from where. The case of the byte[ ] is quite simple: the hard work is already done, and you can simply move on to mapping it in memory, verifying its contents, and working directly with it. However, in the case of a strong name or partial name, there is a bit of work to do initially. The first step is to transform the name into a location. For assembly loads that do not specify version or key information, policy is not consulted. Loads that come from disk or a network location (e.g., Assembly.LoadFrom) that use assemblies with this information will consult policy before fully loading the assembly; this is determined by reading the assembly's manifest. But, for all other loads, no configuration or global assembly cache (GAC) searching is performed.

Consulting the Cache

In the assembly-loading process, before the CLR starts loading any assembly, it will ascertain whether it can reuse an existing assembly. The CLR checks the local cache of the application domain to investigate the previous binding activities. If the CLR discovers that the target assembly has already loaded, it will not start the probing process; it will just reuse that code. Otherwise, the binder proceeds with the process of trying to find a suitable match.

Conclusion

The CLR cannot execute the IL code directly; it needs the assembly. The assembly is a mechanism used by .NET to deploy the application code. In this chapter, you have seen that the assembly has a specific format that is defined in Partition 2 of the ECMA CLR specification. At a very high level the assembly contains information that describes the application code; using predefined headers, the assembly stores the compiled IL code, along with the resource files. The assembly files typically reside in the storage devices, but, as you have already seen, the CPU fetches instructions from the memory. As a result, in order for the CPU to execute, the application code needs to reside in the physical memory. The CLR is responsible for loading the assembly into memory. Understanding how the CLR does this requires knowledge of how the memory works, how the OS manages it, and, most important, how the CLR uses memory. Once you have a solid grasp of memory, you will be able to understand how the CLR handles assembly at runtime. In the next chapter, you will learn about the memory—how it works and how the OS handles it.

Further Reading

Box, Don. *Essential.NET: The Common Language Runtime*. Vol. 1. Boston: Addison-Wesley, 2003.

Jacob, Bruce, Spencer W. Ng, and David T. Wang. *Memory Systems: Cache, DRAM, Disk*. Burlington, MA: Morgan Kaufmann, 2008.

Miller, James S., and Susann Ragsdale. *The Common Language Infrastructure Annotated Standard*. Boston: Addison-Wesley, 2004.

## CHAPTER 4

CLR Memory Model

As you have seen in Chapter 1, the CPU executes instruction by fetching it from the physical memory (RAM). The application code must reside somewhere in the physical memory to be executed by the CPU. It is therefore important that you manage the physical memory while the CPU executes an application. The OS plays a significant role in managing physical memory by abstracting it into a concept called virtual memory. The concept of the virtual memory gives the illusion to the user application that it has a huge range of memory to consume. The OS offers memory management services via the memory API.

The CLR has its own memory abstraction layer, implemented using this memory API, and provides a virtual execution environment for any .NET application. This makes memory operation for the user application easier, and the application developer is not required to write code to access memory, release memory to avoid unexpected memory leak, and so on. The responsibility of managing the memory operations is left to the CLR.

In this chapter, you will focus on the relationship between the OS memory services and the CLR memory model.

Introduction

Physical memory is the range of the physical addresses of the memory cells in which an application or system stores its data, code, and so on during execution. *Memory management* denotes the managing of these physical addresses by swapping the data from physical memory to a storage device and then back to physical memory when needed. The OS implements the memory management services using virtual memory. As a C# application developer you do not need to write any memory management services. The CLR uses the underlying OS memory management services to provide the memory model for C# or any other high-level language targeting the CLR.

Figure 4-1 shows physical memory that has been abstracted and managed by the OS, using the virtual memory concept. Virtual memory is the abstract view of the physical memory, managed by the OS. Virtual memory is simply a series of virtual addresses, and these virtual addresses are translated by the CPU into the physical address when needed.

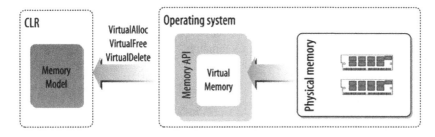

Figure 4-1. *CLR memory abstraction*

The CLR provides the memory management abstract layer for the virtual execution environment, using the operating memory services. The abstracted concepts the CLR uses are AppDomain, thread, stack, heapmemory-mapped file, and so on. The concept of the application domain (AppDomain) gives your application an isolated execution environment.

Memory Interaction between the CLR and OS

By looking at the stack trace while debugging the following C# application, using WinDbg, you will see how the CLR uses the underlying OS memory management services (e.g., the HeapFree method from KERNEL32.dll, the RtlpFreeHeap method from ntdll.dll) to implement its own memory model:

```
using System;

namespace CH_04
{
    class Program
    {
        static void Main(string[] args)
        {
            Book book = new Book();
            Console.ReadLine();
        }
    }

    public class Book
    {
        public void Print() { Console.WriteLine(ToString()); }
    }
}
```

The compiled assembly of the program is loaded into WinDbg to start debugging. You use the following commands to initialize the debugging session:

```
0:000> sxe ld clrjit
0:000> g
0:000> .loadby sos clr
0:000> .load C:\Windows\Microsoft.NET\Framework\v4.0.30319\sos.dll
```

Then, you set a breakpoint at the Main method of the Program class, using the !bpmd command:

```
0:000>!bpmd CH_04.exe   CH_04.Program.Main
```

To continue the execution and break at the breakpoint, execute the g command:

```
0:000> g
```

When the execution breaks at the breakpoint, you use the !eestack command to view the stack trace details of all threads running for the current process. The following output shows the stack trace for all the threads running for the application CH_04.exe:

```
0:000> !eestack
---------------------------------------------
Thread   0
Current frame: (MethodDesc 00233800 +0 CH_04.Program.Main(System.String[]))
ChildEBP RetAddr  Caller, Callee
0022ed24 5faf21db clr!CallDescrWorker+0x33

/*trace removed*/

0022f218 77712d68 ntdll!RtlFreeHeap+0x142, calling ntdll!RtlpFreeHeap
0022f238 771df1ac KERNEL32!HeapFree+0x14, calling ntdll!RtlFreeHeap
0022f24c 5fb4c036 clr!EEHeapFree+0x36, calling KERNEL32!HeapFree
0022f260 5fb4c09d clr!EEHeapFreeInProcessHeap+0x24, calling clr!EEHeapFree
0022f274 5fb4c06d clr!operator delete[]+0x30, calling clr!EEHeapFreeInProcessHeap

/*trace removed*/

0022f4d0 7771316f ntdll!RtlpFreeHeap+0xb7a, calling ntdll!_SEH_epilog4
0022f4d4 77712d68 ntdll!RtlFreeHeap+0x142, calling ntdll!RtlpFreeHeap
0022f4f4 771df1ac KERNEL32!HeapFree+0x14, calling ntdll!RtlFreeHeap

/*trace removed*/
```

This stack trace indicates that the CLR uses OS memory management services to implement its own memory model. Any memory operation in .NET goes via the CLR memory layer to the OS memory management layer.

Figure 4-2 illustrates a typical C# application memory model used by the CLR at runtime.

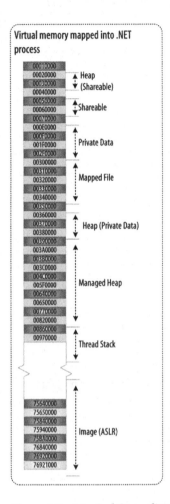

Figure 4-2. *A typical C# application memory model*

The CLR memory model is tightly coupled with the OS memory management services. To understand the CLR memory model, it is important to understand the underlying OS memory model. It is also crucial to know how the physical memory address space is abstracted into the virtual memory address space, the ways the virtual address space is being used by the user application and system application, how virtual-to-physical address mapping works, how memory-mapped file works, and so on. This background knowledge will improve your grasp of CLR memory model concepts, including AppDomain, stack, and heap.

Windows Memory Management

As you learned in Chapter 1, the Windows OS uses the concept of the process to execute different tasks. For example, when you run any C# application, it will run as a process. Moreover, even when Windows itself does anything, it uses the concept of the process to execute.

Concept of the Process

A process is the abstract concept used and implemented by the OS to split systems or application programs among several functional units. The OS achieves this by allocating a separate, private address space for each process. This address space maps resources for the application. For example, the CLR contains the GC, code manager, JIT compiler, and so on. Each of these Windows processes has its own private virtual address space allocated and managed by Windows. When a process is initialized by Windows, it creates a data structure, called the *process environment block (PEB)*, to manage that process, using the OS. When you execute the following application, the OS will create a process to start its execution:

```
using System;

namespace CH_04
{
    class Program
    {
        static void Main(string[] args)
        {
            Console.WriteLine("Process");
        }
    }
    public class Test
    {
        public void TestMethod() { }
    }
}
```

The compiled assembly of this program is loaded into WinDbg to start debugging. To find out more about the process in Windows, you use the !process command in the kernel mode of WinDbg, while the application runs separately. The !process command, with 0 as image name and 0 as Flags, will be shown a list of the processes running in the system at the moment. Among these processes one will be CH_04.exe, as displayed here:

```
lkd> !process 0 0
**** NT ACTIVE PROCESS DUMP ****
PROCESS 8a9f3660 SessionId: none Cid: 0004 Peb: 00000000 ParentCid: 0000
    DirBase: 0b100020 ObjectTable: e1002e00 HandleCount: 2067.
    Image: System

/*removed*/

PROCESS 8545b030 SessionId: 1 Cid: 1050 Peb: 7ffdf000 ParentCid: 14b8
    DirBase: 7ef76620 ObjectTable: dc8291f8 HandleCount: 20.
    Image: CH_04.exe

/*removed*/

PROCESS 88ced330 SessionId: 0 Cid: 07d0 Peb: 7ffdf000 ParentCid: 11dc
    DirBase: 0b100800 ObjectTable: e42b9ef8 HandleCount: 93.
    Image: Windbg
```

!PROCESS 0 0

When using the !process command with Flags as 0, the output will include time and priority statistics; if 0 is used for the process ID, and ImageName is omitted, the debugger displays information about all active processes.

Process Structure

Process is simply a data structure and is manipulated by the OS, based on the specification defined in the OS to manage process. If you examine the process data structure, you will see that it has different fields; some (DirBase, VadRoot, and so on) are used to maintain the address space for that process, as shownhere. You will use the process ID 8672e030, from the previous output, to learn the details of that process, using the !process command, as follows:

```
lkd> !process 84bd4d40 1
PROCESS 84bd4d40 SessionId: 1 Cid: 1650 Peb: 7ffd3000 ParentCid: 14b8
    DirBase: 7ef76620 ObjectTable: db882408 HandleCount: 116.
    Image: CH_04.exe
    VadRoot 85453be8 Vads 70 Clone 0 Private 313. Modified 6. Locked 0.
    DeviceMap 8c463540
    Token                             d9b29c30
    ElapsedTime                       00:01:48.467
    UserTime                          00:00:00.000
    KernelTime                        00:00:00.000
    QuotaPoolUsage[PagedPool]         0
    QuotaPoolUsage[NonPagedPool]      0
    Working Set Sizes (now,min,max)   (1374, 50, 345) (5496KB, 200KB, 1380KB)
    PeakWorkingSetSize                1374
    VirtualSize                       91 Mb
    PeakVirtualSize                   91 Mb
    PageFaultCount                    1415
    MemoryPriority                    BACKGROUND
    BasePriority                      8
    CommitCharge                      1842
    DebugPort                         85d7efc0
```

NOTE

Bit 0 (0x1)Displays time and priority statistics.

Bit 1 (0x2)

Displays a list of threads and events associated with the process and their wait states.

Bit 2 (0x4)

Displays a list of threads associated with the process. If this is included without Bit 1 (0x2), each thread is displayed on a single line. If this is included with Bit 1, each thread is displayed with a stack trace.

Bit 3 (0x8)

(Windows XP and later) Displays the return address, stack pointer, and (on Itanium-based systems) binary space partitioning (BSP) register value for each function. The display of function arguments is suppressed.

Bit 4 (0x10)

(Windows XP and later) Sets the process context equal to the specified process for the duration of this command. This results in a more accurate display of thread stacks. Because this flag is equivalent to using .process /p /r for the specified process, any existing user-mode module list will be discarded. If the process is 0, the debugger displays all processes, and the process context is changed for each one. If you are only displaying a single process, and its user-mode state has already been refreshed (e.g., with .process /p /r), it is not necessary to use this flag. This flag is only effective when used with Bit 0 (0x1).

PROCESS DATA STRUCTURE

If you want to see the complete data structure of the process structure of a process, use the dt command with the structure name and process ID, like this 22:

```
lkd> dt nt!_EPROCESS 84bd4d40
    +0x000 Pcb                         : _KPROCESS
/* removed*/
    +0x16c ImageFileName               : [15] "CH_04.exe"
/* removed*/
    +0x278 VadRoot                     : _MM_AVL_TABLE
    +0x298 AlpcContext                 : _ALPC_PROCESS_CONTEXT
    +0x2a8 TimerResolutionLink         : _LIST_ENTRY [ 0x0 - 0x0 ]
    +0x2b0 RequestedTimerResolution    : 0
    +0x2b4 ActiveThreadsHighWatermark  : 4
    +0x2b8 SmallestTimerResolution     : 0
    +0x2bc TimerResolutionStackRecord  : (null)
```

To view the inner structure, use dt nt!_EPROCESS -b 89733020, in kernel mode.

The dt command displays information about a local variable, global variable, or data type. The !dt command, with the symbol name nt!_EPROCESS, shows the prior information about that e process.

Process Address Space

While studying the output gjven using !process command, you may have noticed a field called DirBase. This field represents the mapping table that mapped the virtual address of the process to the physical address.

You can use the !vad command, with the VadRoot address from the previous output (0x896a9920), to display the virtual address tree associated with that address:

```
lkd> !vad 85453be8
VAD      level    start    end    commit
88f38fe8 ( 3)        10     11         2 Private      READWRITE
/*removed*/
89213460 ( 4)       130    132         0 Mapped       READONLY          Pagefile-backed section
89048cd0 ( 3)       140    140         0 Mapped       READONLY          Pagefile-backed section
88e13298 ( 5)       150    150         1 Private      EXECUTE_READWRITE
89d489a8 ( 4)       160    160         1 Private      READWRITE
```

```
/*removed*/
88e64c70 ( 6)      290     2a5       0 Mapped        READONLY            \WINDOWS\system32\unicode.nls
/*removed*/
897cc728 ( 9)      360     36f       5 Private       READWRITE
892a7ed8 (10)      370     372       0 Mapped        READONLY            \WINDOWS\system32\ctype.nls
893c5550 (11)      380     3bf       3 Private       EXECUTE_READWRITE
8a84d940 (12)      3c0     3c0       0 Mapped        READONLY            Pagefile-backed section
89735de8 (13)      3d0     3dd       0 Mapped        READWRITE           Pagefile-backed section
/*removed*/
894c6e18 ( 1)      400     407       2 Mapped  Exe   EXECUTE_WRITECOPY   \TestApp\TestApp\bin\Debug\TestApp.exe
8a8a54b0 ( 3)      410     4d7       0 Mapped        EXECUTE_READ        Pagefile-backed section
88ed7a10 ( 4)      4e0     5e2       0 Mapped        READONLY            Pagefile-backed section
88ce3110 ( 2)      5f0     8ef       0 Mapped        EXECUTE_READ        Pagefile-backed section
89353230 ( 4)      8f0     8ff       5 Private       READWRITE
88fff088 ( 6)      900     90f       4 Private       READWRITE
88c7f248 ( 5)      910     911       0 Mapped        READONLY            Pagefile-backed section
898a1f68 ( 6)      920     92f       8 Private       READWRITE
8902a9c0 ( 3)      930     93f       5 Private       READWRITE
88cb5480 ( 5)      940     97f       3 Private       EXECUTE_READWRITE
897b8728 ( 6)      980     98f       5 Private       READWRITE
/*removed*/
893c81c0 ( 9)      9b0     9bf       2 Private       NO_ACCESS
892c3998 ( 4)      9c0     9c1       0 Mapped        READONLY            Pagefile-backed section
896a9920 ( 0)      9d0     a0f       3 Private       EXECUTE_READWRITE
88ace740 ( 5)      a10     a1f       3 Private       NO_ACCESS
/*removed*/
89543620 ( 7)      a50     a8f       3 Private       EXECUTE_READWRITE
89603d30 ( 6)      a90     b8f     255 Private       READWRITE
89bca380 ( 7)      b90     c2f     160 Private       WrtWatch READWRITE
898882c8 ( 8)      c30     d2f     253 Private       READWRITE
89b0cfa0 ( 9)      d30     d96       0 Mapped        READONLY
\WINDOWS\Microsoft.NET\Framework\v4.0.30319\locale.nlp
89209238 (10)      da0    1071       0 Mapped        READONLY
\WINDOWS\Microsoft.NET\Framework\v4.0.30319\sortdefault.nlp
889ff388 ( 3)     1120    1121       0 Mapped        READONLY            Pagefile-backed section
892d27b8 ( 4)     1130    312f      36 Private       WrtWatch READWRITE
895f4930 ( 2)    10000   1003a      12 Mapped  Exe   EXECUTE_WRITECOPY   \WINDOWS\system32\sxwmon32.dll
/*removed*/
88e9bb48 ( 4)     7f6f0   7f7ef      0 Mapped        EXECUTE_READ        Pagefile-backed section
88ae66d8 ( 3)     7ffb0   7ffd3      0 Mapped        READONLY            Pagefile-backed section
899242a0 ( 7)     7ffdc   7ffdc      1 Private       READWRITE
/*removed*/

Total VADs: 78, average level: 6, maximum depth: 15
```

Concept of the Thread

A process cannot be executed by the OS directly; it uses another abstract concept, the thread, which works as the execution unit for the functional unit defined by the process. The thread has its own address space, which is a subset of the virtual address space allocated for the process. A thread can only belong to a single process and can only use the resources of that process. A thread includes

- An instruction pointer, which points to the instruction that is currently being executed

- A stack

- A set of register values, defining a part of the state of the processor executing the thread

- A private data region

When a process is created by the OS, it automatically allocates a thread for it, called the main, or primary, thread. It is this thread that executes the runtime host, which in turn loads the CLR.

THREAD ENVIRONMENT BLOCK: !TEB

The CLR maintains the data structure of the thread, as shown:

```
lkd> !teb
TEB at 7ffdf000
    ExceptionList:        0012f440
    StackBase:            00130000
    StackLimit:           0012b000
    SubSystemTib:         00000000
    FiberData:            00001e00
    ArbitraryUserPointer: 00000000
    Self:                 7ffdf000
    EnvironmentPointer:   00000000
    ClientId:             000015b8 . 00001564
    RpcHandle:            00000000
    Tls Storage:          00000000
    PEB Address:          7ffdb000
    LastErrorValue:       0
    LastStatusValue:      c000000f
    Count Owned Locks:    0
    HardErrorMode:        0
```

Here, the thread data structure is displayed in detail, using ?? @$thread or dt nt!_ETHREAD:

```
lkd> ?? @$thread
struct _ETHREAD * 0x88d97760
   +0x000 Tcb               : _KTHREAD
   +0x1c0 CreateTime        : _LARGE_INTEGER 0x0e79ba22`b42e96b8
   +0x1c0 NestedFaultCount  : 0y00
   +0x1c0 ApcNeeded         : 0y0
   +0x1c8 ExitTime          : _LARGE_INTEGER 0x88d97928`88d97928
   +0x1c8 LpcReplyChain     : _LIST_ENTRY [ 0x88d97928 - 0x88d97928 ]
   +0x1c8 KeyedWaitChain    : _LIST_ENTRY [ 0x88d97928 - 0x88d97928 ]
```

```
        +0x1d0 ExitStatus                   : 0n0
        +0x1d0 OfsChain                     : (null)
        +0x1d4 PostBlockList                : _LIST_ENTRY [ 0xe5afc600 - 0xe5c92568 ]
        +0x1dc TerminationPort              : 0xe23f02d8 _TERMINATION_PORT
        +0x1dc ReaperLink                   : 0xe23f02d8 _ETHREAD
        +0x1dc KeyedWaitValue               : 0xe23f02d8 Void
        +0x1e0 ActiveTimerListLock          : 0
        +0x1e4 ActiveTimerListHead          : _LIST_ENTRY [ 0x88d97944 - 0x88d97944 ]
        +0x1ec Cid                          : _CLIENT_ID
        +0x1f4 LpcReplySemaphore            : _KSEMAPHORE
        +0x1f4 KeyedWaitSemaphore           : _KSEMAPHORE
        +0x208 LpcReplyMessage              : (null)
        +0x208 LpcWaitingOnPort             : (null)
        +0x20c ImpersonationInfo            : (null)
        +0x210 IrpList                      : _LIST_ENTRY [ 0x88d97970 - 0x88d97970 ]
        +0x218 TopLevelIrp                  : 0
        +0x21c DeviceToVerify               : (null)
        +0x220 ThreadsProcess               : 0x88ced330 _EPROCESS
        +0x224 StartAddress                 : 0x7c8106f9 Void
        +0x228 Win32StartAddress            : 0x0041f450 Void
        +0x228 LpcReceivedMessageId         : 0x41f450
        +0x22c ThreadListEntry              : _LIST_ENTRY [ 0x8927824c - 0x8895cee4 ]
        +0x234 RundownProtect               : _EX_RUNDOWN_REF
        +0x238 ThreadLock                   : _EX_PUSH_LOCK
        +0x23c LpcReplyMessageId            : 0
        +0x240 ReadClusterSize              : 7
        +0x244 GrantedAccess                : 0x1f03ff
        +0x248 CrossThreadFlags             : 0
        +0x248 Terminated                   : 0y0
        +0x248 DeadThread                   : 0y0
        +0x248 HideFromDebugger             : 0y0
        +0x248 ActiveImpersonationInfo      : 0y0
        +0x248 SystemThread                 : 0y0
        +0x248 HardErrorsAreDisabled        : 0y0
        +0x248 BreakOnTermination           : 0y0
        +0x248 SkipCreationMsg              : 0y0
        +0x248 SkipTerminationMsg           : 0y0
        +0x24c SameThreadPassiveFlags       : 0
        +0x24c ActiveExWorker               : 0y0
        +0x24c ExWorkerCanWaitUser          : 0y0
        +0x24c MemoryMaker                  : 0y0
        +0x250 SameThreadApcFlags           : 0
        +0x250 LpcReceivedMsgIdValid        : 0y0
        +0x250 LpcExitThreadCalled          : 0y0
        +0x250 AddressSpaceOwner            : 0y0
        +0x254 ForwardClusterOnly           : 0 ''
        +0x255 DisableageFaultClustering    : 0 ''
        +0x258 KernelStackReference         : 1
```

The process is the boundary, and the thread is the execution unit that is executed by the CPU. If you explore the details of a process, for example, CH_04.exe, which is executing via the OS, you will discover how many threads are associated with it, as shown:

```
lkd> !process 0 0
**** NT ACTIVE PROCESS DUMP ****
PROCESS 8483a2e8 SessionId: none Cid: 0004 Peb: 00000000 ParentCid: 0000
    DirBase: 00185000 ObjectTable: 89801e28 HandleCount: 649.
    Image: System

/*code removed*/

PROCESS dc406d40 SessionId: 1 Cid: 128c Peb: 7ffd8000 ParentCid: 14b8
    DirBase: 7ef76880 ObjectTable: dbfb9a80 HandleCount: 20.
    Image: CH_04.exe

/*code removed*/
```

The details of the threads associated with CH_04.exe are as follows:

```
lkd> !process dc406d40 4
PROCESS dc406d40 SessionId: 1 Cid: 128c Peb: 7ffd8000 ParentCid: 14b8
    DirBase: 7ef76880 ObjectTable: dbfb9a80 HandleCount: 93.
    Image: CH_04.exe

        THREAD db4fbd48 Cid 128c.1598 Teb: 7ffdf000 Win32Thread: fc08bdd8 WAIT
        THREAD 84a795c8 Cid 128c.130c Teb: 7ffde000 Win32Thread: 00000000 WAIT
        THREAD 8509fd48 Cid 128c.0a10 Teb: 7ffdd000 Win32Thread: 00000000 WAIT
```

Because the OS multitasks, each of the threads in Windows needs to run or be given a time to execute its instructions by the CPU and also to simulate that everything is running simultaneously for a single CPU-based system. The OS ensures this by introducing the concepts of scheduling and the quantum. The quantum is a period of time allocated for each of the threads to use the CPU. To learn the quantum details of all the threads in the process 89961268, debug the application in WinDbg kernel mode while executing the following commands:

```
lkd> !process dc406d40

lkd> ?? @$thread 8947fab8
lkd> ?? @$thread->Tcb
lkd> ?? @$thread->Tcb
struct _KTHREAD
   /*removed*/

   +0x06f Quantum            : 10 ''

   /*removed*/

lkd> ?? @$thread 889ad058
struct _ETHREAD * 0x88d97760
   +0x000 Tcb               : _KTHREAD
/*removed*/
```

```
lkd> ?? @$thread->Tcb
struct _KTHREAD
/*removed*/

   +0x06f Quantum            : 3 ''

   /*removed*/
```

Thread Address Space

As discussed previously, each process has its own address space. Thread is no different in this respect; each of the threads in a process has its own private virtual address space. The thread and virtual address space are shown here:

```
StackBase:              00130000
StackLimit:             0012b000
```

Thread and Frames

A system can have several processes, a process can have many threads, and a thread can have multiple activation frames. The activation frame is a data structure that manages the state of a method while it is executing. A thread begins its life when it is combined with a method as a starting point. To maintain this method call chain, each thread is associated with a set of frames to keep track of the method states.

To get the details of these frames, the .frame command can be used. This command specifies which local context is used by a particular method. The .frame command can take different parameters; /r is shows registers and other information about the specified local context, as displayed here:

```
0:000> .frame /r 01
01 001fe1a8 77720fad ntdll!NtMapViewOfSection+0xc
eax=0c000000 ebx=00000000 ecx=600d9c84 edx=00010001 esi=7ffdf000 edi=001fe290
eip=7770507c esp=001fe1ac ebp=001fe1fc iopl=0         nv up ei pl zr na pe nc
cs=001b ss=0023 ds=0023 es=0023 fs=003b gs=0000            efl=00000246
ntdll!NtMapViewOfSection+0xc:
7770507c c22800           ret     28h
```

Concept of the Virtual Memory

The core function of Windows memory management is to manage the virtual memory. Virtual memory is a conceptual memory model that represents the range of virtual addresses that are mapped to the physical addresses. When any application requires access to memory, the OS allocates the virtual memory for the application. The translation process of the virtual address is supported by the hardware (CPU). When an application program refers to a virtual memory address, the CPU translates it into a physical address. The advantages of accessing memory through a virtual address are as follows:

- *Range of address*: A program can use a contiguous range of virtual addresses to access a large memory buffer that is not contiguous in physical memory.

- *More address space*: A program can use a greater amount of address space, compared with the available physical memory address space. As the supply of physical memory decreases, the memory manager saves pages of it (typically 4 kilobytes) to a disk file. Pages of data or code are moved between physical memory and disk as needed.

- *Isolation address space*: Application programs can use different address space from each other and will be isolated from each other. The code in one process cannot alter the physical memory that is being used by another process.

The range of virtual addresses that can be used by a process is called the virtual address space. The virtual address space can be used in two modes, for example, user mode and kernel mode. Each user-mode process has its own private virtual address space, as does kernel mode. For a 32-bit process the virtual address space is usually 4 gigabytes, and for a 64-bit process, 8 terabytes.

32-bit and 64-bit Process Addressing

A process is a data structure used by the OS to maintain information about it. Each process on 32-bit Microsoft Windows has its own virtual address space that enables addressing up to 4 gigabytes of memory. Each process on 64-bit Windows has a virtual address space of 8 terabytes. All the threads of a process can access their own virtual address space. However, threads cannot access memory that belongs to another process, which protects processes from being corrupted by another process. Figure 4-3 illustrates the addressing scheme used in Windows for 32- and 64-bit installations.

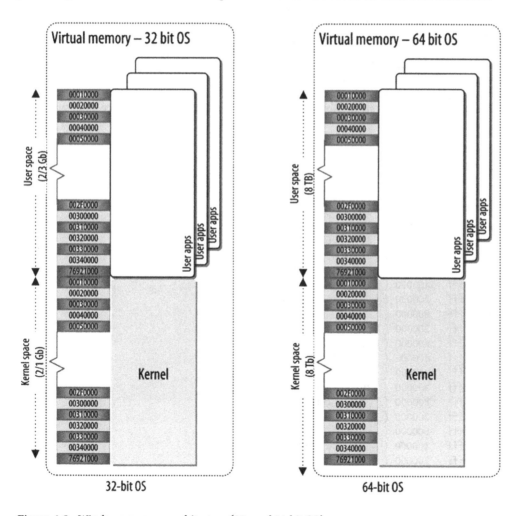

Figure 4-3. *Windows memory architecture (32- and 64-bit OS)*

Windows uses privilege strategy when executing a process. Windows has two modes of execution, based on classification by privilege level: user mode and kernel mode. Typically, user mode is less privileged than kernel mode.

Some examples of user-mode applications are the applications provided in this book, drivers, and so on; examples of kernel mode are all the core OS components.

In Windows all processes run in isolation to eliminate the potential for a system crash; if one application crashes while executing, the rest of the system can keep working. This multiprocess execution environment is possible because of the use of isolated address space for each process.

Applications run in isolation as well. If an application crashes, the system will not stop working, and neither other applications nor the OS is affected.

The Windows OS in 32-bit mode can support up to 4 gigabytes of addressable virtual space. Of this space, 2 gigabytes are used by the user-mode application, and 2 gigabytes, by the kernel itself. A user-mode application can get up to 3 gigabytes, and kernel mode, 1 gigabyte of address space when the extended user application memory is enabled in the system.

The 64-bit Windows OS addressable memory space is shared between active applications and the kernel. The kernel address space includes a system page table entry (PTE) area (kernel memory thread stacks), paged pool (page tables, kernel objects), system cache (file cache, registry), and Nonpaged pool (images, and so on).

The default 64-bit Windows OS configuration provides up to 16 terabytes (2^54) of addressable memory space, divided equally between the kernel and the user applications; with 16 terabytes of physical memory available, 8 terabytes of virtual address space are allocated to the kernel, and 8 terabytes, to user application memory. The kernel virtual address space is shared across processes. Each 64-bit process has its own space, whereas each 32-bit application runs in a virtual 2 gigabyte Windows-on-Windows (WOW).

The kernel address space includes a system PTE area (kernel memory thread stacks), paged pool (page tables, kernel objects), system cache (file cache, registry), and nonpaged pool (images, and so on). You have seen how VMMap shows the user application's address space. Now, let's look at the kernel-mode address space and how the OS allocates it:

###	Start	End	Length (	MB)	Count	Type
001	80000000	803fffff	400000 (	4)	2	BootLoaded
002	80400000	807fffff	400000 (	4)	2	SystemPtes
003	80800000	81dfffff	1600000 (	22)	11	BootLoaded
004	81e00000	827fffff	a00000 (	10)	5	PagedPool
005	82800000	839fffff	1200000 (	18)	9	BootLoaded
006	83a00000	845fffff	c00000 (	12)	6	PfnDatabase
007	84600000	851fffff	c00000 (	12)	6	NonPagedPool
008	85200000	853fffff	200000 (	2)	1	SystemCache
009	85400000	867fffff	1400000 (	20)	10	NonPagedPool
010	86800000	869fffff	200000 (	2)	1	PagedPool
011	86a00000	871fffff	800000 (	8)	4	SystemCache
012	87200000	873fffff	200000 (	2)	1	SystemPtes
013	87400000	87dfffff	a00000 (	10)	5	SystemCache
014	87e00000	881fffff	400000 (	4)	2	PagedPool
015	88200000	885fffff	400000 (	4)	2	SystemCache
016	88600000	88ffffff	a00000 (	10)	5	DriverImages
017	89000000	897fffff	800000 (	8)	4	BootLoaded
018	89800000	899fffff	200000 (	2)	1	PagedPool
019	89a00000	89ffffff	600000 (	6)	3	SystemPtes
020	8a000000	8a3fffff	400000 (	4)	2	SystemCache
021	8a400000	8a5fffff	200000 (	2)	1	SystemPtes
022	8a600000	8a7fffff	200000 (	2)	1	SystemCache
023	8a800000	8a9fffff	200000 (	2)	1	PagedPool
024	8aa00000	8abfffff	200000 (	2)	1	SystemPtes
025	8ac00000	8c3fffff	1800000 (	24)	12	SystemCache

```
026  8c400000   8c5fffff   200000 (    2)    1 PagedPool
027  8c600000   8c7fffff   200000 (    2)    1 SystemPtes
028  8c800000   8d3fffff   c00000 (   12)    6 SystemCache
029  8d400000   8d5fffff   200000 (    2)    1 DriverImages
030  8d600000   8d7fffff   200000 (    2)    1 SystemCache
031  8d800000   8dbfffff   400000 (    4)    2 PagedPool
032  8dc00000   8ddfffff   200000 (    2)    1 DriverImages
033  8de00000   8dffffff   200000 (    2)    1 SystemCache
034  8e000000   8e9fffff   a00000 (   10)    5 DriverImages
035  8ea00000   8ebfffff   200000 (    2)    1 SystemPtes
036  8ec00000   8f3fffff   800000 (    8)    4 SystemCache
037  8f400000   8f5fffff   200000 (    2)    1 PagedPool
038  8f600000   8f9fffff   400000 (    4)    2 SystemCache
039  8fa00000   8fbfffff   200000 (    2)    1 PagedPool
040  8fc00000   911fffff  1600000 (   22)   11 SystemCache
041  91200000   915fffff   400000 (    4)    2 PagedPool
042  91600000   917fffff   200000 (    2)    1 SystemCache
043  91800000   923fffff   c00000 (   12)    6 PagedPool
044  92400000   925fffff   200000 (    2)    1 SystemCache
045  92600000   931fffff   c00000 (   12)    6 PagedPool
046  93200000   933fffff   200000 (    2)    1 SystemCache
047  93400000   93ffffff   c00000 (   12)    6 PagedPool
048  94000000   941fffff   200000 (    2)    1 SystemCache
049  94200000   94dfffff   c00000 (   12)    6 PagedPool
050  94e00000   94ffffff   200000 (    2)    1 SystemCache
051  95000000   955fffff   600000 (    6)    3 PagedPool
052  95600000   959fffff   400000 (    4)    2 SystemCache
053  95a00000   95bfffff   200000 (    2)    1 DriverImages
054  95c00000   95dfffff   200000 (    2)    1 SystemPtes
055  95e00000   961fffff   400000 (    4)    2 SystemCache
056  96200000   963fffff   200000 (    2)    1 DriverImages
057  96400000   965fffff   200000 (    2)    1 PagedPool
058  96600000   969fffff   400000 (    4)    2 SystemCache
059  96a00000   96bfffff   200000 (    2)    1 SystemPtes
060  96c00000   977fffff   c00000 (   12)    6 SessionGlobalSpace
061  97800000   97bfffff   400000 (    4)    2 SystemCache
062  97c00000   97ffffff   400000 (    4)    2 PagedPool
063  98000000   99ffffff  2000000 (   32)   16 SystemPtes
064  9a000000   9a3fffff   400000 (    4)    2 SystemCache
065  9a400000   9a5fffff   200000 (    2)    1 PagedPool
066  9a600000   9a7fffff   200000 (    2)    1 DriverImages
067  9a800000   9b5fffff   e00000 (   14)    7 SystemCache
068  9b600000   9b7fffff   200000 (    2)    1 PagedPool
069  9b800000   9bbfffff   400000 (    4)    2 SystemCache
070  9bc00000   9bdfffff   200000 (    2)    1 PagedPool
071  9be00000   9d1fffff  1400000 (   20)   10 SystemCache
072  9d200000   9d3fffff   200000 (    2)    1 DriverImages
073  9d400000   9d5fffff   200000 (    2)    1 PagedPool
074  9d600000   9edfffff  1800000 (   24)   12 SystemCache
075  9ee00000   9effffff   200000 (    2)    1 PagedPool
076  9f000000   a07fffff  1800000 (   24)   12 SystemCache
```

077	a0800000	a09fffff	200000	(2)	1	PagedPool
078	a0a00000	a0bfffff	200000	(2)	1	SystemCache
079	a0c00000	a0dfffff	200000	(2)	1	SystemPtes
080	a0e00000	a21fffff	1400000	(20)	10	SystemCache
081	a2200000	a23fffff	200000	(2)	1	PagedPool
082	a2400000	a25fffff	200000	(2)	1	SystemCache
083	a2600000	a31fffff	c00000	(12)	6	PagedPool
084	a3200000	a33fffff	200000	(2)	1	SystemCache
085	a3400000	a35fffff	200000	(2)	1	SystemPtes
086	a3600000	a39fffff	400000	(4)	2	PagedPool
087	a3a00000	a5bfffff	2200000	(34)	17	SystemCache
088	a5c00000	a5dfffff	200000	(2)	1	SystemPtes
089	a5e00000	a79fffff	1c00000	(28)	14	SystemCache
090	a7a00000	a7bfffff	200000	(2)	1	PagedPool
091	a7c00000	a7fffff	400000	(4)	2	SystemCache
092	a8000000	a83fffff	400000	(4)	2	PagedPool
093	a8400000	a89fffff	600000	(6)	3	SystemCache
094	a8a00000	a8dfffff	400000	(4)	2	PagedPool
095	a8e00000	a8fffff	200000	(2)	1	SystemCache
096	a9000000	a91fffff	200000	(2)	1	PagedPool
097	a9200000	a9bfffff	a00000	(10)	5	SystemCache
098	a9c00000	a9dfffff	200000	(2)	1	PagedPool
099	a9e00000	aa9fffff	c00000	(12)	6	SystemCache
100	aaa00000	aabfffff	200000	(2)	1	PagedPool
101	aac00000	ab9fffff	e00000	(14)	7	SystemCache
102	aba00000	abbfffff	200000	(2)	1	PagedPool
103	abc00000	ad3fffff	1800000	(24)	12	SystemCache
104	ad400000	ad5fffff	200000	(2)	1	PagedPool
105	ad600000	ae3fffff	e00000	(14)	7	SystemCache
106	ae400000	ae5fffff	200000	(2)	1	SystemPtes
107	ae600000	aedfffff	800000	(8)	4	SystemCache
108	aee00000	af7fffff	a00000	(10)	5	PagedPool
109	af800000	af9fffff	200000	(2)	1	SystemPtes
110	afa00000	affffff	600000	(6)	3	SystemCache
111	b0000000	b01fffff	200000	(2)	1	PagedPool
112	b0200000	b1dfffff	1c00000	(28)	14	SystemCache
113	b1e00000	b1ffffff	200000	(2)	1	PagedPool
114	b2000000	bfffffff	e000000	(224)	112	Unused
115	c0000000	c0ffffff	1000000	(16)	8	ProcessSpace
116	c1000000	fc3fffff	3b400000	(948)	474	Unused
117	fc400000	fc5fffff	200000	(2)	1	SessionSpace
118	fc600000	fc9fffff	400000	(4)	2	Unused
119	fca00000	ffbfffff	3200000	(50)	25	SessionSpace
120	ffc00000	ffffffff	400000	(4)	2	Hal

RANGE OF VIRTUAL ADDRESS SPACE

You can use the poi command in WinDbg kernel mode to explore the virtual address space used by your system. The ?poi command takes its symbol name from the relevant output its implementation yields. In this example, nt!MmHighestUserAddress and nt!mmhighestuseraddress are used to investigate the range of virtual memory for your system:

```
lkd> ?poi(nt!MmHighestUserAddress)
Evaluate expression: 2147418111 = 7ffeffff

lkd> dp nt!mmhighestuseraddress L1
82ba5714  7ffeffff
```

This output indicates that the user space ranges from the address 0x00000000 to 0x7FFEFFFF; the system space therefore ranges from 0x80000000 to the highest possible address (which is 0xFFFFFFFF on a standard 32-bit Windows installation).

As discussed previously, each virtual memory allocated for a process is mapped to the physical memory by the OS. The implementation details of this mapping are hidden, but you can use WinDbg to study the mapping during the execution of a C# application.

Virtual-to-Physical Address Mapping

Each virtual address of a process is mapped to a physical memory address This mapping is managed by the OS. The following C# program can be used to study how the virtual address is mapped to physical memory at runtime:

```csharp
using System;
namespace CH_04
{
    class Program
    {
        static void Main(string[] args)
        {
            Console.WriteLine("Virtual to Physical address mappings");
            Console.ReadLine();
        }
    }
}
```

Once the program is compiled, run it, opening it with WinDbg, in kernel mode, to explore the virtual-to-physical address mappings. In the kernel mode of WinDbg, you will execute the !process command, with the process value as 0 and the flags value as 0, to view currently running processes in the system, as shown:

```
lkd> !process 0 0
**** NT ACTIVE PROCESS DUMP ****
PROCESS 8483a2e8  SessionId: none  Cid: 0004    Peb: 00000000  ParentCid: 0000
    DirBase: 00185000  ObjectTable: 89801e28  HandleCount: 642.
    Image: System
```

```
/*process removed*/
PROCESS 84ae14f8 SessionId: 1 Cid: 0b44 Peb: 7ffda000 ParentCid: 14b8
    DirBase: 7ef76820 ObjectTable: e006df68 HandleCount: 20.
    Image: CH_04.exe

/*process removed*/
```

Each of the processes from the prior output has a set of elements to describe the process, such as Process ID, PEB, and DirBase. The DirBase element specifies the directory base for the relevant process. This directory base contains mapping between virtual and physical memory. You will use the !ptov command in WinDbgkernel mode. The !ptov command displays the entire physical-to-virtual memory map for a given process. You will be using the process ID 7ec6f2e0 as a parameter of the !ptov command to display the entire physical-to-virtual memory address mapping for the process 7ec6f2e0.

```
!ptov 7ef76820
/*mapping removed*/

69676000      94632000
d077000       94633000
dff9000       94635000
7d1fa000      94636000
300bb000      94637000
4dc3c000      94638000
388af000      94639000

/*mapping removed*/

0             ffd0b000
106000        ffd0c000

/*mapping removed*/

fee00000      fffe0000
```

The address on the left-hand side is the physical address of each memory page that has a mapping for this process. The address on the right-hand side is the virtual address used by the application.

Learn the Contents of a Particular Physical Memory Address

You can use the !dc command to view the contents of the physical address and the dc command to show the contents of the Virtual address. Therefore, from the previous physical-to-virtual memory mapping, you looked at a physical address and its corresponding virtual address to see whether the contents of these memory addresses are same or not. You also used the !dc command with a physical address as a parameter, and a virtual address as a parameter with the dc command to view the memory contents. Technically, the physical address and virtual memory address will have the same contents, as the virtual address is mapped to the physical address.

```
lkd> !dc 106000
#   106000 ffd09000 ffd07000 7fee3180 00000000 .....p...1......
#   106010 54445344 00003955 4247ef01 20202054 DSDTU9....GBT
#   106020 55544247 49504341 00001000 5446534d GBTUACPI....MSFT
#   106030 0100000c 5c054310 5f52505f 5c11835b .....C.\_PR_[..\
#   106040 52505f2e 5550435f 04100030 5b060000 ._PR_CPU0......[
#   106050 2e5c1183 5f52505f 31555043 00041001 ..\._PR_CPU1....
#   106060 835b0600 5f2e5c11 435f5250 02325550 ..[..\._PR_CPU2.
#   106070 00000410 11835b06 505f2e5c 50435f52 .....[..\._PR_CP
```

```
lkd> dc ffd0c000
ffd0c000  ffd09000 ffd07000 7fee3180 00000000  .....p...1......
ffd0c010  54445344 00003955 4247ef01 20202054  DSDTU9....GBT
ffd0c020  55544247 49504341 00001000 5446534d  GBTUACPI....MSFT
ffd0c030  0100000c 5c054310 5f52505f 5c11835b  .....C.\_PR_[..\
ffd0c040  52505f2e 5550435f 04100030 5b060000  ._PR_CPU0......[
ffd0c050  2e5c1183 5f52505f 31555043 00041001  ..\._PR_CPU1....
ffd0c060  835b0600 5f2e5c11 435f5250 02325550  ..[..\._PR_CPU2.
ffd0c070  00000410 11835b06 505f2e5c 50435f52  .....[..\._PR_CP
```

Furthermore, you used the physical address 106000 as a parameter with the !dc command, and the corresponding virtual address ffd0c000 as a parameter with the dc command, to display the memory contents. Both addresses show the same memory contents, as they refer to the same memory cell.

Find a Virtual Address and Its Contents

Now, you will compile the program, using the C# compiler (csc.exe), and load it into WinDbg for debugging to find a virtual address. Later, you will use that virtual address to examine the program's contents.

```csharp
using System;

namespace CH_04
{
    class Program
    {
        static void Main(string[] args)
        {
            Console.WriteLine("Virtual to Physical address mappings");
        }
    }
}
```

The compiled assembly of this program is loaded into WinDbg to begin debugging. You will be using the following commands to initialize the debugging session:

```
0:000> sxe ld clrjit
0:000> g
0:000> .loadby sos clr
0:000> .load C:\Windows\Microsoft.NET\Framework\v4.0.30319\sos.dll
```

You will find a virtual memory address during this debugging session and use that address as the start address for dumping the contents of the memory. Then, you will go downward from the start address, to 100, to use as the end address of the range.

To achieve this, you set a breakpoint, using the !bpmd command at the Main method of the Program class:

```
0:000> !bpmd CH_04.exe CH_04.Program.Main
```

Then, you continue with the execution, using the g command, which will break when it hits the Main method, as shown:

```
0:000> g
(b44.11e8): CLR notification exception - code e0444143 (first chance)
JITTED CH_04!CH_04.Program.Main(System.String[])
Setting breakpoint: bp 003B0070 [CH_04.Program.Main(System.String[])]
Breakpoint 0 hit
eax=002437f0 ebx=00000000 ecx=019db674 edx=001eed90 esi=00297910 edi=001eece0
eip=003b0070 esp=001eecb8 ebp=001eecc4 iopl=0         nv up ei pl nz ac pe nc
cs=001b ss=0023 ds=0023 es=0023 fs=003b gs=0000            efl=00000216
003b0070 55              push    ebp
```

This output gives the contents of the registers' values, along with other information. You will use the memory address stored in the EIP register to view the contents of this memory. This address will be used as the base for a range, spanning from the start address to 100. Next, you use the dd command to display the contents of the memory for the given range; theywill display as double-worded values, like this:

```
0:000> dd 002437f0-100
002436f0   00000000 00000000 00000000 00000000
00243700   00000000 00000000 00000000 00000000
00243710   00000000 00000000 00000000 00000000
00243720   00000000 00000000 00000000 00000000
00243730   00000000 00000000 00000000 00000000
00243740   00000000 00000000 00000000 00000000
00243750   00000000 00000000 029d1ff4 00000000
00243760   029d1ff8 00000000 5fb13a20 00000004
```

The left-hand column from this memory dump provides the start address of the memory, followed by the contents of that location.

Memory-Mapped File

Typically, when you reference any virtual memory to access its contents, it will go to the physical memory, based on the virtual-to-physical mapping table, where, as in the memory-mapped file, instead of seeking the physical memory, it will look for the physical file, which has been mapped as a memory-mapped file, with the range of the virtual addresses in the process address space.

Thus, accessing the content of a memory-mapped file is just a dereferencing of an address from the mapped virtual memory, which will seek the contents of the address in the memory-mapped physical file stored in the storage device (see Figure 4-4).

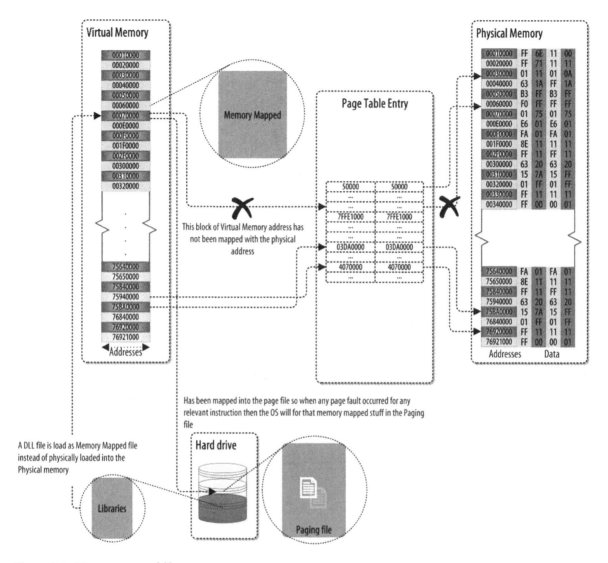

Figure 4-4. *Memory-mapped file*

For example, let's say the range of virtual addresses from your process address space 10000 to 15000 has been mapped as a memory-mapped file in the storage device `MemoryMappedFile.txt`. Thus, if you want to access the contents of the virtual memory 10005, the memory management services of the OS will go to the `MemoryMappedFile.txt` file and seek the region of the file that has been mapped as 10001.

Now, let's look at the output for a control area used for this process. This output shows how the memory-mapped file has been handled and maintained by the OS. The following C# program will be compiled, using csc.exe, and then loaded into WinDbg to see whether any memory-mapped file is used by the CLR at runtime to execute the program:

```
using System;
namespace CH_04
{
    class Program
    {
        static void Main(string[] args)
        {
            Book book = new Book();
        }
    }

    public class Book { }
}
```

The compiled assembly of the program is loaded into WinDbg to start debugging. Next, you use these commands to initialize the debugging session:

```
0:000> sxe ld clrjit
0:000> g
0:000> .loadby sos clr
0:000> .load C:\Windows\Microsoft.NET\Framework\v4.0.30319\sos.dll
```

Then, you set a breakpoint, using !bpmd, and let the execution continue, using g, until hitting the specified breakpoint:

```
0:000> !bpmd CH_04.exe CH_04.Book.Print
Found 1 methods in module 00412e9c...
Adding pending breakpoints...
0:000> !bpmd CH_04.exe CH_04.Program.Main
Found 1 methods in module 00412e9c...
MethodDesc = 00413800
Adding pending breakpoints...

0:000> g
```

After applying the g command, you use the frame command, with r parameters, to display the registers and other information about the current local context:

```
(ca4.e40): CLR notification exception - code e0444143 (first chance)
JITTED CH-04!CH_04.Program.Main(System.String[])
Setting breakpoint: bp 004D0070 [CH_04.Program.Main(System.String[])]
Breakpoint 0 hit
eax=00413800 ebx=00000000 ecx=0196b77c edx=002bf0f0 esi=000f8e60 edi=002bf040
eip=004d0070 esp=002bf018 ebp=002bf024 iopl=0         nv up ei pl nz ac pe nc
cs=001b ss=0023 ds=0023 es=0023 fs=003b gs=0000              efl=00000216
004d0070 55                  push    ebp
```

Next, you use the !address command to identify the memory address the target process uses. The !address command has f parameters, which can take different filter values to allow display of only particular regions' address space for a given address.

Now, you will explore the mapped file, using !address /f:FILE_MAP, as shown:

```
0:000> !address -f:FileMap

Mapping file section regions...
Mapping module regions...
Mapping PEB regions...
Mapping TEB and stack regions...
Mapping heap regions...
Mapping page heap regions...
Mapping other regions...
Mapping stack trace database regions...
Mapping activation context regions...


BaseAddr  EndAddr+1  RgnSize      Type        State         Protect               Usage
-----------------------------------------------------------------------------------------------
80000      81000     1000    MEM_MAPPED   MEM_COMMIT   PAGE_READWRITE   MappedFile "PageFile"
90000      a0000     10000   MEM_MAPPED   MEM_COMMIT   PAGE_READWRITE   MappedFile "PageFile"
2c0000     327000    67000   MEM_MAPPED   MEM_COMMIT   PAGE_READONLY    MappedFile "\Device\
HarddiskVolume7\Windows\System32\locale.nls"
4a0000     4b0000    10000   MEM_MAPPED   MEM_COMMIT   PAGE_READONLY    MappedFile "PageFile"
4b0000     560000    b0000   MEM_MAPPED   MEM_RESERVE                   MappedFile "PageFile"
560000     563000    3000    MEM_MAPPED   MEM_COMMIT   PAGE_READONLY    MappedFile "PageFile"
563000     568000    5000    MEM_MAPPED   MEM_RESERVE                   MappedFile "PageFile"
930000     ab2000    182000  MEM_MAPPED   MEM_COMMIT   PAGE_READONLY    MappedFile "PageFile"
ab2000     1530000   a7e000  MEM_MAPPED   MEM_RESERVE                   MappedFile "PageFile"
3a70000    3d3f000   2cf000  MEM_MAPPED   MEM_COMMIT   PAGE_READONLY    MappedFile "\Device\
HarddiskVolume7\Windows\Globalization\Sorting\SortDefault.nls"
3d40000    4012000   2d2000  MEM_MAPPED   MEM_COMMIT   PAGE_READONLY    MappedFile "\Device\
HarddiskVolume7\Windows\Microsoft.NET\Framework\v4.0.30319\sortdefault.nlp"
7f6f5000   7f7f0000  fb000   MEM_MAPPED   MEM_RESERVE                   MappedFile "PageFile"
```

Memory-mapped files and how they work—nice description of the memory mapped files provided here:

```
0:000> !vmmap
Start      Stop       Length    AllocProtect  Protect   State    Type
00000000-0000ffff   00010000                  NA        Free
00010000-0001ffff   00010000   RdWr           RdWr      Commit   Mapped
00020000-0002ffff   00010000   RdWr           RdWr      Commit   Mapped
00030000-00033fff   00004000   Rd             Rd        Commit   Mapped
00034000-0003ffff   0000c000                  NA        Free
00040000-00040fff   00001000   Rd             Rd        Commit   Mapped
```

Here, the virtual memory has already been mapped as a memory-mapped file. It is maintained using the data structure _CONTROL_AREA:

```
lkd> dt nt!_CONTROL_AREA
   +0x000 Segment                    : Ptr32 _SEGMENT
   +0x004 DereferenceList            : _LIST_ENTRY
   +0x00c NumberOfSectionReferences  : Uint4B
   +0x010 NumberOfPfnReferences      : Uint4B
   +0x014 NumberOfMappedViews        : Uint4B
   +0x018 NumberOfSubsections        : Uint2B
   +0x01a FlushInProgressCount       : Uint2B
   +0x01c NumberOfUserReferences     : Uint4B
   +0x020 u                          : __unnamed
   +0x024 FilePointer                : Ptr32 _FILE_OBJECT
   +0x028 WaitingForDeletion         : Ptr32 _EVENT_COUNTER
   +0x02c ModifiedWriteCount         : Uint2B
   +0x02e NumberOfSystemCacheViews   : Uint2B
```

You use the !memusage command, from WinDbg, to see how the virtual memory is mapped:

```
lkd> !memusage
 loading PFN database
loading (100% complete)
Compiling memory usage data (99% Complete).
            Zeroed:  16041 ( 64164 kb)
              Free:      4 (    16 kb)
           Standby: 148360 (593440 kb)
          Modified:  36405 (145620 kb)
   ModifiedNoWrite:    180 (   720 kb)
       Active/Valid: 317051 (1268204 kb)
        Transition:   5132 ( 20528 kb)
               Bad:    729 (  2916 kb)
           Unknown:      0 (     0 kb)
             TOTAL: 523173 (2092692 kb)
  Building kernel map
  Finished building kernel map
Scanning PFN database - (100% complete)

  Usage Summary (in Kb):
Control  Valid Standby Dirty Shared Locked PageTables  name
 1fffffd  3108       0     0      0      0        0  AWE
86770608   308      32     0      0      0        0  mapped_file( Siyamrupali.ttf )
84a8f148     0     380     0      0      0        0  mapped_file( msmincho.ttc )
84c076f8 16928    3908     0  14852      0        0  mapped_file( chrome_child.dll )
8581d850  4012    5812     0      0      0        0  mapped_file( $Mft )
86896818   184    1024     0      0      0        0  mapped_file( 1.TXT )
8569c8f0  5640   26460     0      0      0        0  mapped_file( $LogFile )
84c2ea88   128    9300     0      0      0        0  mapped_file( data_1 )
85771168  1888    2156     0      0      0        0  mapped_file( No name for file )
84cbf5f8   108     236     0      0      0        0  mapped_file( Visited Links )
```

To obtain the details of this mapping, you investigate the control, using the !ca command, which will give you the inner workings of the memory-mapped mapping mechanism in Windows:

```
lkd> !ca 86896818

ControlArea @ 86896818
  Segment       97c0ea80  Flink       00000000  Blink          00000000
  Section Ref           1  Pfn Ref         16a  Mapped Views          2
  User Ref              0  WaitForDel        0  Flush Count           0
  File Object  868b5be8  ModWriteCount      0  System Views          2
  WritableRefs          0
  Flags (c080) File WasPurged Accessed

       \1.TXT

Segment @ 97c0ea80
  ControlArea 86896818 ExtendInfo    00000000
  Total Ptes 200
  Segment Size 200000 Committed            0
  Flags (c0000) ProtectionMask

Subsection 1 @ 86896868
  ControlArea  86896818  Starting Sector       0  Number Of Sectors  100
  Base Pte     9b891008  Ptes In Subsect     100  Unused Ptes          0
  Flags               d  Sector Offset         0  Protection           6
  Accessed
  Flink        84efa224  Blink            84a70cbc  MappedViews         0

Subsection 2 @ 84de7e38
  ControlArea  86896818  Starting Sector     100  Number Of Sectors  100
  Base Pte     86eb5000  Ptes In Subsect     100  Unused Ptes        100
  Flags               d  Sector Offset         0  Protection           6
  Accessed
  Flink        00000000  Blink            00000000  MappedViews         2
```

MEMORY REGIONS DISPLAYED

- *VAR*: Busy regions. These regions include all virtual allocation blocks, the small block heap (SBH), memory from custom allocators, and regions of the address space that fall under no other classification.

- *Free*: Free memory. This includes all memory that has not been reserved.

- *Image*: Memory that is mapped to a file that is part of an executable image.

- *Stack*:Memory used for thread stacks.

- *Teb*: Memory used for thread environment blocks (TEBs).

- *Peb*: Memory used for the PEB.

- *Heap*: Memory used for heaps.

- *PageHeap*: The memory region used for the full-page heap.

- *CSR* : CSR-shared memory.

- *Actx*: Memory used for activation context data.

- NLS: Memory used for national language support (NLS) tables.

- *FileMap*: Memory used for memory-mapped files. This filter is applicable only during live debugging.

Conclusion

physical memory (RAM) is the place where the application program, including OS executable instruction, is loaded during execution. The CPU fetches instruction from the memory and executes. The OS is responsible for handling and managing the physical memory and provides memory management services, using the concepts of virtual memory and API to access those services. The API is capable of allocating, deallocating, querying, and deleting memory from the physical memory via the memory management layer. Most of the programming languages targeting the Windows OS have their own memory model, implemented with Windows memory management services, unless they explicitly implement their own memory management layer to access physical memory directly.

In .NET the virtual execution environment the CLR implements its own memory abstraction layer, using the Windows virtual memory management services. In this chapter you learned how Windows manages and handles memory. In the next chapter, you will consider the memory abstraction layer used by the CLR. The CLR uses the abstraction concept of the application domain to start execution of a .NET application. The application domain is the combination of the virtual address space and specification implemented in the CLR. This specification indicates how to deal with the range of the virtual memory, and so on. Inside the application domain the CLR lays out other abstract concepts, such as managed thread, stack, and heap.

Further Reading

Farrell, Chris, and Nick Harrison. *Under the Hood of .NET Memory Management*. S.l., Simple Talk.

Hewardt, Mario. *Advanced .NET Debugging*. Upper Saddle River, NJ: Addison-Wesley, 2010.

Hewardt, Mario, and Daniel Pravat, D. *Advanced Windows Debugging*. Upper Saddle River, NJ: Addison-Wesley, 2008.

Jacob, Bruce, Spencer W. Ng, and David T. Wang. *Memory Systems: Cache, DRAM, Disk*. Burlington, MA: Morgan Kaufmann, 2010.

Juola, Patrick. *Principles of Computer Organization and Assembly Language*. Upper Saddle River, NJ: Prentice Hall, 2007.

Lidin, Serge. *Inside Microsoft: NET IL Assembler*. Redmond, WA: Microsoft.

McDougall, Richard, and Jim Mauro. *Solaris Internals: Solaris 10 and OpenSolaris Kernel Architecture*. Upper Saddle River, NJ: Prentice Hall, 2006.

Pratschner, Steven. *Customizing the Microsoft .NET Framework Common Language Runtime*. Edited by Kathleen Atkins. Redmond, WA: Microsoft, 2009.

CHAPTER 5

■ ■ ■

CLR Memory Model II

In Chapter 4, you learned about Windows memory management. The CLR uses the underlying Windows memory management services to implement its own memory model to provide memory to the user's application. In this chapter, you will explore the CLR memory model to learn different concepts used in the CLR. You will look at the application domain and how the CLR structures and allocates virtual memory for it. You will also examine other contexts, such as Stack and Heap.

CLR Memory Model: Application Domain

In the CLR an application domain is used to isolate the execution boundary for security, versioning, reliability, and unloading of the managed code. An application domain by itself cannot be executed by the CLR, which serves as the container to hold the application. At runtime the CLR loads all the managed code of an application into one or more application domains and executes that code, using one or more threads (thread is a mechanism used by the OS to execute application code by the CPU; see Chapters 1 and 4).

There is not a one-to-one mapping between application domains and threads. At runtime a single application domain can be used to execute multiple threads, but a particular thread is not restricted to executing in a single application domain. In the CLR, threads have the capability to cross application domain boundaries, and multiple threads can be executed in any given application domain.

The CLR is responsible for keeping track of threads and the application domain relationship. The following C# application can be used to explore the relationship between application domain and thread:

```
using System;

namespace CH_05
{
    class Program
    {
        static void Main(string[] args)
        {
            Book book = new Book();
            book.Print();
        }
    }

    public class Book
    {
        public void Print() { Console.WriteLine(ToString()); }
    }
}
```

Once this application is compiled into an assembly (CH_05.exe), using csc.exe, you load this assembly into WinDbg to start debugging. You will be using the following command to initialize the debugging session:

```
0:000> sxe ld clrjit
0:000> g
0:000> .loadby sos clr
0:000> .load C:\Windows\Microsoft.NET\Framework\v4.0.30319\sos.dll
```

Next, set a break point, using the !bpmd command, and then let the execution continue, using the g command:

```
0:000> !name2ee CH_05.exe CH_05.Program.Main
Module:       00292e9c
Assembly:     CH_05.exe
Token:        06000001
MethodDesc:   00293800
Name:         CH_05.Program.Main(System.String[])
Not JITTED yet. Use !bpmd -md 00293800 to break on run.


0:000>!bpmd -md 00293800
0:000> g
```

The !threads command, along with the -live option, can be used to see all the running threads for this executable:

```
0:000> !threads -live
ThreadCount:      2
UnstartedThread:  0
BackgroundThread: 1
PendingThread:    0
DeadThread:       0
Hosted Runtime:   no
```

	ID	OSID	ThreadOBJ	State	PreEmptive GC	GC Alloc Context	Domain	Lock Count	APT	Exception
0	1	1370	002c78e8	a020	Enabled	0166b684:0166c004	002c1078	2	MTA	
2	2	1660	003017c0	b220	Enabled	00000000:00000000	002c1078	0	MTA	(Finalizer)

As you can see, the output offers information about domain. To find the domain, you can use the !dumpdomain command, as follows:

```
0:000> !dumpdomain 002c1078
--------------------------------------
Domain 1:           002c1078
LowFrequencyHeap:   002c13f4
HighFrequencyHeap:  002c1440
StubHeap:           002c148c
Stage:              OPEN
SecurityDescriptor: 002c27f0
Name:               CH_05.exe
Assembly:           003033c0 [C:\Windows\Microsoft.Net\assembly\GAC_32\mscorlib\
v4.0_4.0.0.0__b77a5c561934e089\mscorlib.dll]
ClassLoader:        00303460
SecurityDescriptor: 0030af20
  Module Name
```

```
55d81000          C:\Windows\Microsoft.Net\assembly\GAC_32\mscorlib\v4.0_4.0.0.0__b77a5c561934e089\
mscorlib.dll

Assembly:          003135d8 [J:\Book\C# Deconstructed\SourceCode\Chapters\CH_05\bin\Debug\CH_05.exe]
ClassLoader:       00313678
SecurityDescriptor: 00312c00
  Module Name
00292e9c           J:\Book\C# Deconstructed\SourceCode\Chapters\CH_05\bin\Debug\CH_05.exe
```

The CLR uses its own memory model while executing a .NET application. The CLR begins its execution by allocating application domains for the .NET application. The application domain concept provides manageable, isolated, secure structure for the .NET application at runtime.

The application domain is a combination of a data structure that has a virtual address space and specification regarding how to manipulate that virtual address space to isolate the execution state of each application domain in a process. Figure 5-1 displays a block of virtual addresses that have been allocated for different application domains, such as System Domain, Shared Domain, and Default Domain.

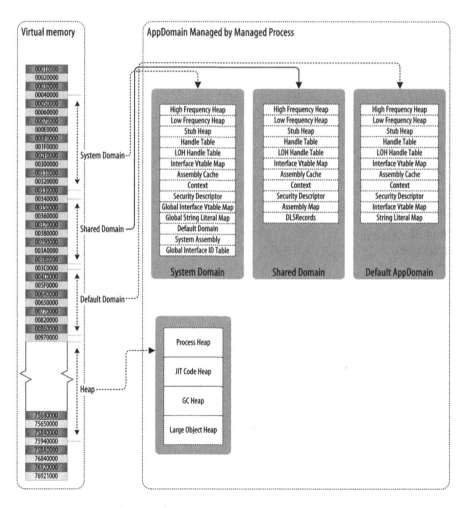

Figure 5-1. *CLR application domain*

The CLR allocates three default application domains, such as System Domain, Shared Domain, and Default Domain, during the execution of an assembly. You can explore these application domains while debugging a C# application via WinDbg. The following example can be used to reveal the different application domains used by this assembly:

```
using System;

namespace CH_05
{
    class Program
    {
        static void Main(string[] args)
        {
            Book book = new Book();
            book.Print();
        }
    }

    public class Book
    {
        public void Print() { Console.WriteLine(ToString()); }
    }
}
```

Once this application is compiled into an assembly (CH_05.exe), using csc.exe, you load the assembly into WinDbg to start debugging. You will be using the following command to initialize the debugging session:

```
0:000> sxe ld clrjit
0:000> g
0:000> .loadby sos clr
0:000> .load C:\Windows\Microsoft.NET\Framework\v4.0.30319\sos.dll
```

Next, set a break point, using the !bpmd command, and then let the execution continue, using the g command:

```
0:000> !bpmd CH_05.exe CH_05.Program.Main
Found 1 methods in module 00232e9c...
MethodDesc = 00233800
Adding pending breakpoints...

0:000> !bpmd CH_05.exe CH_05.Book.Print
Found 1 methods in module 00232e9c...
Adding pending breakpoints...
```

The g command will continue the execution of the program until it hits the break point:

```
0:000> g
(fe8.1308): CLR notification exception - code e0444143 (first chance)
JITTED CH_05!CH_05.Program.Main(System.String[])
Setting breakpoint: bp 004A0070 [CH_05.Program.Main(System.String[])]
Breakpoint 0 hit
eax=00233800 ebx=00000000 ecx=0198b674 edx=0020f070 esi=002b78e8 edi=0020efc0
eip=004a0070 esp=0020ef98 ebp=0020efa4 iopl=0         nv up ei pl nz ac po nc
cs=001b  ss=0023  ds=0023  es=0023  fs=003b  gs=0000              efl=00000212
004a0070 55              push    ebp
```

The !dumpdomain command can be used to show the domain details of the program. When !dumpdomain is used with no parameters, it will list all AppDomain objects of the running process, as shown:

```
0:000> !dumpdomain
--------------------------------------
System Domain:      58cd2478
LowFrequencyHeap:   58cd2784
HighFrequencyHeap:  58cd27d0
StubHeap:           58cd281c
Stage:              OPEN
Name:               None
--------------------------------------
Shared Domain:      58cd2140
LowFrequencyHeap:   58cd2784
HighFrequencyHeap:  58cd27d0
StubHeap:           58cd281c
Stage:              OPEN
Name:               None
Assembly:           002f4368 [C:\Windows\Microsoft.Net\assembly\GAC_32\mscorlib\v4.0_4.0.0.0__
b77a5c561934e089\mscorlib.dll]
ClassLoader:        002f4408
Module Name
56fc1000            C:\Windows\Microsoft.Net\assembly\GAC_32\mscorlib\v4.0_4.0.0.0__b77a5c561934e089\
mscorlib.dll


--------------------------------------
Domain 1:           002b1078
LowFrequencyHeap:   002b13f4
HighFrequencyHeap:  002b1440
StubHeap:           002b148c
Stage:              OPEN
SecurityDescriptor: 002b27f0
Name:               CH_05.exe
Assembly:           002f4368 [C:\Windows\Microsoft.Net\assembly\GAC_32\mscorlib\v4.0_4.0.0.0__
b77a5c561934e089\mscorlib.dll]
ClassLoader:        002f4408
SecurityDescriptor: 002f4138
Module Name
56fc1000            C:\Windows\Microsoft.Net\assembly\GAC_32\mscorlib\
v4.0_4.0.0.0__b77a5c561934e089\mscorlib.dll

Assembly:           00302110 [J:\Book\C# Deconstructed\SourceCode\Chapters\CH_05\bin\Debug\CH_05.exe]
ClassLoader:        00301240
SecurityDescriptor: 002fe4f8
Module Name
00232e9c            J:\Book\C# Deconstructed\SourceCode\Chapters\CH_05\bin\Debug\CH_05.exe
```

As mentioned earlier, the application domain is a range of virtual addresses where the CLR stores application-related information at runtime. For example, Stack will be allocated for a region of the application domain, Heap will be stored in the application, and so on. When an object is instantiated during application execution, the CLR will store that object in a specific region of the application domain.

Finding an object in the Application Domain

To find an object in the application domain, you will use the same debugging session as in the previous section. In that debugging session the execution pointer was set in the Main method. Now, you will apply the g command to continue the execution, but, because you set the break point at Print method, you will halt it at Print method:

```
0:000> g
(fe8.1308): CLR notification exception - code e0444143 (first chance)
JITTED CH_05!CH_05.Book.Print()
Setting breakpoint: bp 004A0110 [CH_05.Book.Print()]
Breakpoint 1 hit
eax=0023386c ebx=00000000 ecx=0198b684 edx=002b78e8 esi=002b78e8 edi=0020efc0
eip=004a0110 esp=0020ef84 ebp=0020ef94 iopl=0         nv up ei pl nz ac po nc
cs=001b  ss=0023  ds=0023  es=0023  fs=003b  gs=0000            efl=00000212
004a0110 55               push    ebp
```

Then, execute the following command:

```
0:000> !clrstack -a
OS Thread Id: 0x1370 (0)
Child SP IP       Call Site
0016ed84 00440110 CH_05.Book.Print()*** WARNING: Unable to verify checksum for CH_05.exe
  [J:\Book\C# Deconstructed\SourceCode\Chapters\CH_05\Program.cs @ 16]
    PARAMETERS:
        this (<CLR reg>) = 0x0166b684

0016ed88 004400b4 CH_05.Program.Main(System.String[]) [J:\Book\C# Deconstructed\SourceCode\Chapters\
CH_05\Program.cs @ 10]
    PARAMETERS:
        args (0x0016ed90) = 0x0166b674
    LOCALS:
        0x0016ed8c = 0x0166b684

0016efc8 56b521db [GCFrame: 0016efc8]
```

The !clrstack command is used to show the current stack trace, From the Parameters section of the prior output, you can find the address of an object, such as 0x0198b684. To discover where this object resides, use the !findappdomain command, as shown:

```
0:000> !findappdomain 0x0166b684
AppDomain: 002c1078
Name:      CH_05.exe
ID:        1
```

You can reveal the relevant domain information like so:

```
0:000> !dumpdomain 002c1078
--------------------------------------
Domain 1:            002c1078
LowFrequencyHeap:    002c13f4
HighFrequencyHeap:   002c1440
StubHeap:            002c148c
Stage:               OPEN
SecurityDescriptor:  002c27f0
Name:                CH_05.exe
Assembly:            003033c0 [C:\Windows\Microsoft.Net\assembly\GAC_32\mscorlib\v4.0_4.0.0.0__
b77a5c561934e089\mscorlib.dll]
ClassLoader:         00303460
SecurityDescriptor:  0030af20
Module Name
55d81000             C:\Windows\Microsoft.Net\assembly\GAC_32\mscorlib\v4.0_4.0.0.0__b77a5c561934e089\
mscorlib.dll

Assembly:            003135d8 [J:\Book\C# Deconstructed\SourceCode\Chapters\CH_05\bin\Debug\CH_05.exe]
ClassLoader:         00313678
SecurityDescriptor:  00312c00
  Module Name
00292e9c             J:\Book\C# Deconstructed\SourceCode\Chapters\CH_05\bin\Debug\CH_05.exe
```

Address Space of the Application Domain

In Windows, process and thread maintain their own address space. A similar concept is used with .NET for the application domain. The CLR allocates an address space for each of the application domains while executing an application. Once a .NET application is loaded into the memory to execute, the CLR allocates virtual address space for that application, using the concept of the application domain, and maintains this address space in the process data structure for the application (see Figure 5-2). Later, the OS maps those virtual addresses in the physical memory as needed.

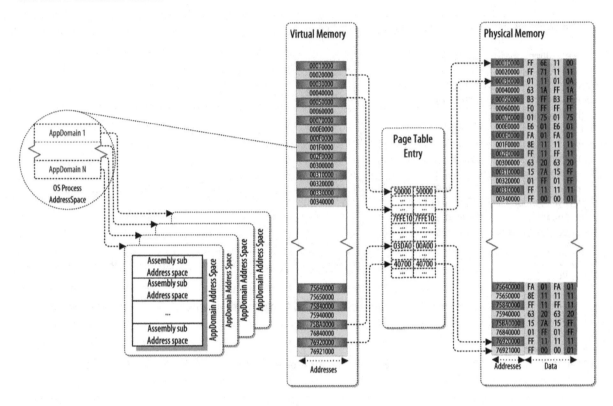

Figure 5-2. *CLR address space*

Let's look at the following example, which you will be using to examine the address space allocated by the CLR for a C# application:

```
using System;

namespace CH_05
{
    class Program
    {
        static void Main(string[] args)
        {
        }
    }
}
```

Once this application is compiled into an assembly (CH_05.exe), using csc.exe, you will load the assembly into WinDbg to start debugging. You will be using the following command to initialize the debugging session:

```
0:000> sxe ld clrjit
0:000> g
0:000> .loadby sos clr
0:000> .load C:\Windows\Microsoft.NET\Framework\v4.0.30319\sos.dll
```

The !eeheap command, along with the -loader option, can be used to display the range of the virtual addresses allocated for the different domains of an application. The following output gives the address space of the prior application:

```
0:000> !eeheap -loader
Loader Heap:
--------------------------------------
System Domain:     58cd2478
LowFrequencyHeap:  001b0000(2000:1000) Size: 0x1000 (4096) bytes.
HighFrequencyHeap: 001b2000(8000:1000) Size: 0x1000 (4096) bytes.
StubHeap:          001ba000(2000:1000) Size: 0x1000 (4096) bytes.
Virtual Call Stub Heap:
  IndcellHeap:     00360000(2000:1000) Size: 0x1000 (4096) bytes.
  LookupHeap:      00365000(2000:1000) Size: 0x1000 (4096) bytes.
  ResolveHeap:     0036b000(5000:1000) Size: 0x1000 (4096) bytes.
  DispatchHeap:    00367000(4000:1000) Size: 0x1000 (4096) bytes.
  CacheEntryHeap:  Size: 0x0 (0) bytes.
Total size:        Size: 0x7000 (28672) bytes.
--------------------------------------
Shared Domain:     58cd2140
LowFrequencyHeap:  001b0000(2000:1000) Size: 0x1000 (4096) bytes.
HighFrequencyHeap: 001b2000(8000:1000) Size: 0x1000 (4096) bytes.
StubHeap:          001ba000(2000:1000) Size: 0x1000 (4096) bytes.
Virtual Call Stub Heap:
  IndcellHeap:     00360000(2000:1000) Size: 0x1000 (4096) bytes.
  LookupHeap:      00365000(2000:1000) Size: 0x1000 (4096) bytes.
  ResolveHeap:     0036b000(5000:1000) Size: 0x1000 (4096) bytes.
  DispatchHeap:    00367000(4000:1000) Size: 0x1000 (4096) bytes.
  CacheEntryHeap:  Size: 0x0 (0) bytes.
Total size:        Size: 0x7000 (28672) bytes.
--------------------------------------
Domain 1:          00201078  ♥
LowFrequencyHeap:  001c0000(2000:2000) Size: 0x2000 (8192) bytes.
HighFrequencyHeap: 001c2000(8000:2000) Size: 0x2000 (8192) bytes.
StubHeap:          Size: 0x0 (0) bytes.
Virtual Call Stub Heap:
  IndcellHeap:     Size: 0x0 (0) bytes.
  LookupHeap:      Size: 0x0 (0) bytes.
  ResolveHeap:     Size: 0x0 (0) bytes.
  DispatchHeap:    Size: 0x0 (0) bytes.
  CacheEntryHeap:  Size: 0x0 (0) bytes.
Total size:        Size: 0x4000 (16384) bytes.
--------------------------------------
Jit code heap:
Total size:        Size: 0x0 (0) bytes.
--------------------------------------
Module Thunk heaps:
Module 56fc1000:   Size: 0x0 (0) bytes.
Module 001c2e9c:   Size: 0x0 (0) bytes.
Total size:        Size: 0x0 (0) bytes.
```

```
----------------------------------------
Module Lookup Table heaps:
Module 56fc1000:        Size: 0x0 (0) bytes.
Module 001c2e9c:        Size: 0x0 (0) bytes.
Total size:             Size: 0x0 (0) bytes.
----------------------------------------
Total LoaderHeap size:  Size: 0x12000 (73728) bytes.
========================================
```

Stack in the CLR

When the CLR executes any method, it uses *local storage* for that method. This local storage is a range of the virtual addresses allocated from the Stack region of the application domain. The Stack is also a range of virtual addresses that are part of the application domain allocated to use as Stack for the application. The CLR uses parts of this Stack address space as local storage for a method while executing it.

The life of the local storage of a method begins when the CLR is about to execute that method. Local storage is simply a special convention for handling a range of virtual addresses. The CLR populates the local storage during execution of the method, for instance, populating the Parameters section with data passed as parameters for the method. The CLR stores local variables of the method in the Locals section of the method stack.

Here is an example that will help explain the concept of the Stack. Here, the Program class instantiates an instance of the Book class and calls the Test_1 method from the instance of the Book class. Then, the Test_1 method calls Test_2, Test_2 calls Test_3, Test_3 calls Test_4, Test_4 calls Test_5, and Test_5 calls Test_6, as shown:

```
using System;

namespace CH_05
{
    class Program
    {
        static void Main(string[] args)
        {
            Book book = new Book();
            book.Test_1();
            Console.ReadLine();
        }
    }

    public class Book
    {
        public void Test_1() { int i = 0; Console.WriteLine(++i); Test_2(); }
        public void Test_2() { int i = 1; Console.WriteLine(++i); Test_3(); }
        public void Test_3() { int i = 2; Console.WriteLine(++i); Test_4(); }
        public void Test_4() { int i = 3; Console.WriteLine(++i); Test_5(); }
        public void Test_5() { int i = 4; Console.WriteLine(++i); Test_6(); }
        public void Test_6() { int i = 5; Console.WriteLine(++i); }
    }
}
```

The life of the Test_1 method will start while executing the Main method as the Test_1 method is called from it. Before the CLR begins executing the Test_1 method, it will allocate the range of virtual addresses from the Stack region address space to the Test_1 method to use as the local storage for that method. When the local storage address space is allocated to the Test_1 method, it will use that address space to store its parameters, local variables, and so on. If you want to explore this further, compile the preceding program, and debug, using the WinDbg tool.

Once this application is compiled into an assembly (CH_05.exe), using csc.exe, you load the assembly into WinDbg to start debugging. You will be using the following command to initialize the debugging session:

```
0:000> sxe ld clrjit
0:000> g
0:000> .loadby sos clr
0:000> .load C:\Windows\Microsoft.NET\Framework\v4.0.30319\sos.dll
```

By debugging the program, you will find out more about the stack while the CLR executes the program on a thread from the process:

```
0:000> !bpmd CH_05.exe CH_05.Program.Main
Found 1 methods in module 00142e9c...
Adding pending breakpoints...


0:000> !bpmd CH_05.exe CH_05.Book.Test_6
Found 1 methods in module 00142e9c...
Adding pending breakpoints...
```

Let the execution continue, using the g command:

g

The execution will break at the break point, which, in this case, is the Main method. You will execute the g command again to let the execution continue and break at the Test_6 method. Then, you will execute the !clrstack command, along with the parameter -a, to show arguments to the managed method and information on local variables:

```
0:000> !clrstack -a
OS Thread Id: 0x124c (0)
Child SP IP       Call Site
0016f234 004002a0 CH_05.Book.Test_6() [J:\Book\C# Deconstructed\SourceCode\Chapters\CH_05\Program.cs @ 22]
    PARAMETERS:
        this (<CLR reg>) = 0x018ab684
    LOCALS:
        <no data>

0016f238 00400289 CH_05.Book.Test_5() [J:\Book\C# Deconstructed\SourceCode\Chapters\CH_05\Program.cs @ 21]
    PARAMETERS:
        this (0x0016f238) = 0x018ab684
    LOCALS:
        0x0016f23c = 0x00000005

0016f248 00400239 CH_05.Book.Test_4() [J:\Book\C# Deconstructed\SourceCode\Chapters\CH_05\Program.cs @ 20]
    PARAMETERS:
        this (0x0016f248) = 0x018ab684
    LOCALS:
        0x0016f24c = 0x00000004
```

```
0016f258 004001e9 CH_05.Book.Test_3() [J:\Book\C# Deconstructed\SourceCode\Chapters\CH_05\Program.cs @ 19]
    PARAMETERS:
        this (0x0016f258) = 0x018ab684
    LOCALS:
        0x0016f25c = 0x00000003

0016f268 00400199 CH_05.Book.Test_2() [J:\Book\C# Deconstructed\SourceCode\Chapters\CH_05\Program.
cs @ 18]
    PARAMETERS:
        this (0x0016f268) = 0x018ab684
    LOCALS:
        0x0016f26c = 0x00000002

0016f278 00400147 CH_05.Book.Test_1() [J:\Book\C# Deconstructed\SourceCode\Chapters\CH_05\Program.
cs @ 17]
    PARAMETERS:
        this (0x0016f278) = 0x018ab684
    LOCALS:
        0x0016f27c = 0x00000001

0016f288 004000b4 CH_05.Program.Main(System.String[]) [J:\Book\C# Deconstructed\SourceCode\Chapters\
CH_05\Program.cs @ 10]
    PARAMETERS:
        args (0x0016f290) = 0x018ab674
    LOCALS:
        0x0016f28c = 0x018ab684

0016f4c0 5d3a21db [GCFrame: 0016f4c0]
```

From the preceding WinDbg output, you can see how Test_1, Test_2, Test_3, Test_4, Test_5, and Test_6 stack up on each other. The CLR will manage method state on each method call and store in the Stack region allocated for the application. Figure 5-3 shows that the Main method sits at the bottom of the stack, as it is the initiator of the method call chain, and Test_6 is the top of the stack, as this is where the method chain ends.

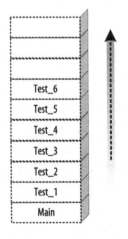

Figure 5-3. *CLR stack model*

Each method state stores information related to that method, such as current execution state (e.g., IL using the IP). In addition, each method state contains Parameters and Locals sections, in which it stores incoming arguments and the local variables it uses.

Once the program is executed by the CLR, the CLR maintains the method call, as demonstrated in Figure 5-4.

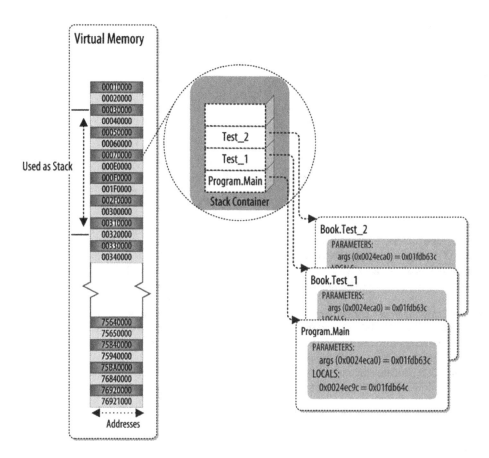

Figure 5-4. *Virtual address space and the Stack*

The CLR is responsible for using the Stack concept to maintain the method state. The method-calling convention in the CLR is stack based, and the methods called are stacked up on each other. Once a method has finished its execution, it is removed from the top of the stack by the CLR, as shown in Figure 5-5.

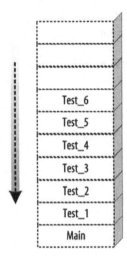

Figure 5-5. *CLR frame execution*

The life of the local storage for a method ends when the method finishes its execution. In constrast, the CLR will maintain the local storage of that method when the current method calls another method to execute. Until that method finishes, the CLR keeps the local storage alive for the caller method. For example, if the CLR executes method A, and method A then calls method B, until method B finishes the execution, the CLR will keep alive the local storage for method A.

The CLR is responsible for using the Stack concept while executing the methods. For example, as mentioned earlier, the CLR executes method by method while executing an application. A method will call the CLR, using a data structure called an activation frame to capture the method execution state and return information. This activation frame is the data structure that virtually refers to local storage.

As discussed previously, the CLR allocates the range of virtual addresses from the application domain address space to use as the Stack. In the following section, you will study the Stack address space allocated by the CLR while executing the example program.

Address Space of the Stack

As mentioned earlier, the Stack is simply a range of virtual memory addresses and the rules specified in the CLR to handle them. If you apply the following command while debugging the previous executable, using WinDbg, you will find that a range of virtual addresses is defined as the Stack. In WinDbg the !address command, along with the -summary option, can be used to display the virtual memory allocated for the executable:

```
0:000> !address -summary

Mapping file section regions...
Mapping module regions...
Mapping PEB regions...
Mapping TEB and stack regions...
Mapping heap regions...
Mapping page heap regions...
Mapping other regions...
```

```
Mapping stack trace database regions...
Mapping activation context regions...

/*removed*/
Stack                                  1691000           fc000 (1008.000 kb)
/*removed*/
```

In WinDbg, using the !address command, along with the /f:Stack flag, will show you more information about the Stack, such as size, range of virtual addresses allocated for the Stack block, and so on:

```
0:000> !address /f:STACK
```

BaseAddr	EndAddr+1	RgnSize	Type	State	Protect	Usage
110000	111000	1000	MEM_PRIVATE	MEM_RESERVE		Stack
[~0; d7c.1018]						
111000	209000	f8000	MEM_PRIVATE	MEM_COMMIT	PAGE_READWRITE	Stack
[~0; d7c.1018]						
209000	20b000	2000	MEM_PRIVATE	MEM_COMMIT	PAGE_READWRITE|PAGE_GUARD	Stack
[~0; d7c.1018]						
20b000	210000	5000	MEM_PRIVATE	MEM_COMMIT	PAGE_READWRITE	Stack
[~0; d7c.1018]						
1690000	1691000	1000	MEM_PRIVATE	MEM_RESERVE		Stack
[~1; d7c.1334]						
1691000	178d000	fc000	MEM_PRIVATE	MEM_COMMIT	PAGE_READWRITE	Stack
[~1; d7c.1334]						
178d000	178f000	2000	MEM_PRIVATE	MEM_COMMIT	PAGE_READWRITE|PAGE_GUARD	Stack
[~1; d7c.1334]						
178f000	1790000	1000	MEM_PRIVATE	MEM_COMMIT	PAGE_READWRITE	Stack
[~1; d7c.1334]						
38b0000	38b1000	1000	MEM_PRIVATE	MEM_RESERVE		Stack
[~2; d7c.e4c]						
38b1000	38b2000	1000	MEM_PRIVATE	MEM_COMMIT	PAGE_READWRITE	Stack
[~2; d7c.e4c]						
38b2000	38b4000	2000	MEM_PRIVATE	MEM_COMMIT	PAGE_READWRITE|PAGE_GUARD	Stack
[~2; d7c.e4c]						
38b4000	39ac000	f8000	MEM_PRIVATE	MEM_COMMIT	PAGE_READWRITE	Stack
[~2; d7c.e4c]						
39ac000	39ae000	2000	MEM_PRIVATE	MEM_COMMIT	PAGE_READWRITE|PAGE_GUARD	Stack
[~2; d7c.e4c]						
39ae000	39b0000	2000	MEM_PRIVATE	MEM_COMMIT	PAGE_READWRITE	Stack
[~2; d7c.e4c]						

```
???
```

Heap

In .NET the heap is used to store all the reference types, such as

- Classes

- Interfaces

- Delegates

- Strings

- Instances of objects

The CLR stores the instances of the reference types in either the large object heap (LOH) or the small object heap (SOH), depending on the size of the objects. When the CLR instantiates any reference type, it instantiates on the heap and assigns the reference type an address. This address is used to access that object later on (the object address from the Stack region of the application can be used). In this example the reference type TestClass has been instantiated to execute the Method_1 of that type:

```
using System;

namespace CH_05
{
    class Program
    {
        static void Main(string[] args)
        {
            TestClass testClass = new TestClass();
            testClass.Method_1();
            Console.ReadLine();
        }
    }

    public class TestClass
    {
        public void Method_1() { }
    }
}
```

The CLR will instantiate an instance of the TestClass while executing the Main method. During the TestClass type instantiation the CLR allocates a block of virtual memory in which to lay out that type, which is referred to as an object. The first address in the memory block will be used to refer to this object. The address can be used from the location where the instantiation process of that type is triggered, such as the Main method. You can also pass around this address to refer to the object in your application.

When you debugged the prior application, using WinDbg, the CLR stored on the local storage of the Main method an address (0x0184b64c), which is the address of the instance of the TestClass. This address refers to the memory block in which the CLR lays out out the instance of the TestClass.

To investigate this further, you can debug the executable produced by the preceding code in windbg.exe. While debugging, using WinDbg, you will set the break point at Main method and Method_1, using the !bpmd command, and let the execution continue, using the g command. During this execution the execution will break at Method_1. Next, will you run the !clrstack command, which will give you information about the Locals section of the Main method and Method_1 method. The Locals section of the Main method contains an address for the TestClass class variable, as shown:

```
0:000> !clrstack -a
OS Thread Id: 0x14fc (0)
Child SP IP    Call Site
002ff024 004e0110 CH_05.TestClass.Method_1() [J:\Book\C# Deconstructed\SourceCode\Chapters\CH_05\
Program.cs @ 17]
    PARAMETERS:
        this (<CLR reg>) = 0x018ab684

002ff028 004e00b4 CH_05.Program.Main(System.String[]) [J:\Book\C# Deconstructed\SourceCode\Chapters\
CH_05\Program.cs @ 10]
    PARAMETERS:
        args (0x002ff030) = 0x018ab674
    LOCALS:
        0x002ff02c = 0x018ab684

002ff26c 5d3a21db [GCFrame: 002ff26c]
```

As discussed previously, whenever an object has been instantiated by the CLR, the CLR allocates a block of virtual addresses from the Heap region of that application domain. You can use the !dumpheap command to find out whether the object instantiated for the preceding program is located in the Heap region:

```
0:000> !dumpheap -mt 0x018ab674
Address      MT     Size
01b3b684 0x018ab674   12
total 0 objects
Statistics:
     MT    Count    TotalSize Class Name
00143880       1          12 CH_05.TestClass
Total 1 objects
```

As with the Stack region, the CLR allocates a range of the virtual addresses from the application domain address space to use as the Heap. In the following section, you will explore the Heap address space allocated by the CLR while executing the program.

Heap and Address Space

In WinDbg you can use the !address, command, along with the /f:Heap flag, to show more information about Heap, such as size, range of virtual addresses allocated for the Heap block, and so on:

```
0:000> !address /f:HEAP
```

BaseAddr	EndAddr+1	RgnSize	Type	State	Protect	Usage
10000	20000	10000	MEM_MAPPED	MEM_COMMIT	PAGE_READWRITE	Heap
[ID: 1; Handle: 00010000; Type: Segment]						
20000	30000	10000	MEM_MAPPED	MEM_COMMIT	PAGE_READWRITE	Heap
[ID: 2; Handle: 00020000; Type: Segment]						
e0000	e3000	3000	MEM_PRIVATE	MEM_COMMIT	PAGE_READWRITE	Heap
[ID: 3; Handle: 000e0000; Type: Segment]						
e3000	f0000	d000	MEM_PRIVATE	MEM_RESERVE		Heap
[ID: 3; Handle: 000e0000; Type: Segment]						
260000	263000	3000	MEM_PRIVATE	MEM_COMMIT	PAGE_READWRITE	Heap
[ID: 6; Handle: 00260000; Type: Segment]						
263000	270000	d000	MEM_PRIVATE	MEM_RESERVE		Heap
[ID: 6; Handle: 00260000; Type: Segment]						
270000	2d4000	64000	MEM_PRIVATE	MEM_COMMIT	PAGE_READWRITE	Heap
[ID: 0; Handle: 00270000; Type: Segment]						
2d4000	370000	9c000	MEM_PRIVATE	MEM_RESERVE		Heap
[ID: 0; Handle: 00270000; Type: Segment]						
4e0000	4e1000	1000	MEM_PRIVATE	MEM_COMMIT	PAGE_EXECUTE_READWRITE	Heap
[ID: 4; Handle: 004e0000; Type: Segment]						
4e1000	520000	3f000	MEM_PRIVATE	MEM_RESERVE		Heap
[ID: 4; Handle: 004e0000; Type: Segment]						
660000	661000	1000	MEM_PRIVATE	MEM_COMMIT	PAGE_EXECUTE_READWRITE	Heap
[ID: 7; Handle: 00660000; Type: Segment]						
661000	6a0000	3f000	MEM_PRIVATE	MEM_RESERVE		Heap
[ID: 7; Handle: 00660000; Type: Segment]						
700000	703000	3000	MEM_PRIVATE	MEM_COMMIT	PAGE_READWRITE	Heap
[ID: 5; Handle: 00700000; Type: Segment]						
703000	710000	d000	MEM_PRIVATE	MEM_RESERVE		Heap
[ID: 5; Handle: 00700000; Type: Segment]						
1400000	1401000	1000	MEM_PRIVATE	MEM_COMMIT	PAGE_EXECUTE_READWRITE	Heap
[ID: 9; Handle: 01400000; Type: Segment]						
1401000	1440000	3f000	MEM_PRIVATE	MEM_RESERVE		Heap
[ID: 9; Handle: 01400000; Type: Segment]						
14e0000	14e1000	1000	MEM_PRIVATE	MEM_COMMIT	PAGE_EXECUTE_READWRITE	Heap
[ID: 10; Handle: 014e0000; Type: Segment]						
14e1000	1520000	3f000	MEM_PRIVATE	MEM_RESERVE		Heap
[ID: 10; Handle: 014e0000; Type: Segment]						
1520000	1523000	3000	MEM_PRIVATE	MEM_COMMIT	PAGE_READWRITE	Heap
[ID: 8; Handle: 01520000; Type: Segment]						
1523000	1530000	d000	MEM_PRIVATE	MEM_RESERVE		Heap
[ID: 8; Handle: 01520000; Type: Segment]						

objects

An *object* is a data structure that has different fields that describe the instance of a type. The address of an object is a location in the virtual memory that points to a block of virtual memory addresses used by the CLR to lay out a type. The contents of that memory block contain the definition of the object. At runtime the virtual memory allocated for the object is mapped in the physical memory (see Chapter 4).

Figure 5-6 shows how an object is loaded into the physical memory and the layout itself, based on the allocation of virtual memory.

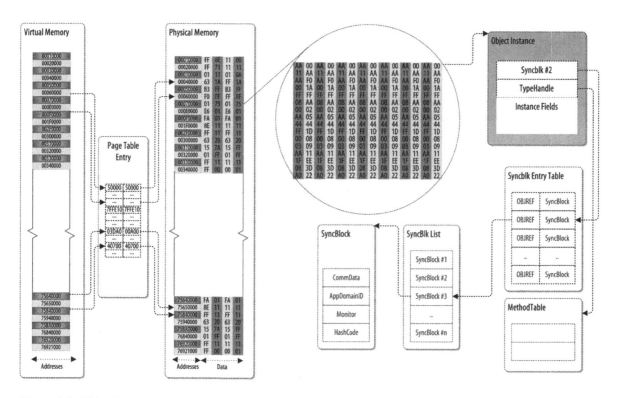

Figure 5-6. *Object instance*

The block of virtual memory addresses is used to define an object data structure. The virtual memory block allocated for an object starts with header information. Here, the header contains a few elements, including Syncblk, which points to the Synblk Entry Table. This table has a list of the Syncblock. The object header also has the MethodTable, which contains all the methods defined in the type and inherited from the base type. You will use the following example to further explore the object in the C# application:

```
using System;

namespace CH_05
{
    class Program
    {
        static void Main(string[] args)
```

```
        {
            Book book = new Book();
            book.Print();
        }
    }

    public class Book
    {
        public void Print()
        {
            Console.WriteLine(ToString());
        }
    }
}
```

Once this application is compiled into an assembly (CH_05.exe), using csc.exe, you will load this assembly into WinDbg to start debugging. You will use the following commands to initialize the debugging session:

```
0:000> sxe ld clrjit
0:000> g
0:000> .loadby sos clr
0:000> .load C:\Windows\Microsoft.NET\Framework\v4.0.30319\sos.dll
```

Let the execution continue, using the g command, after setting the break point:

```
0:000> !bpmd CH_05.exe CH_05.Program.Main
Found 1 methods in module 00342e9c...
MethodDesc = 00343800
Adding pending breakpoints...

0:000> !bpmd CH_05.exe CH_05.Book.Print
Found 1 methods in module 00342e9c...
Adding pending breakpoints...

0:000> g
(15e8.139c): CLR notification exception - code e0444143 (first chance)
JITTED CH_05!CH_05.Book.Print()
Setting breakpoint: bp 003F0110 [CH_05.Book.Print()]
Breakpoint 1 hit
eax=0034386c ebx=00000000 ecx=01f7b684 edx=000878e8 esi=000878e8 edi=002ceda0
eip=003f0110 esp=002ced64 ebp=002ced74 iopl=0         nv up ei pl nz ac pe nc
cs=001b  ss=0023  ds=0023  es=0023  fs=003b  gs=0000              efl=00000216
003f0110 55              push    ebp
```

When you execute the g command, it will continue the execution and stop at the break point (in this case, the Print method). The Main method keeps track of the object in its Local Variables section, which can be used to further study the object structure. If you execute the !clrstack command, along with the a option, it will show the current execution state of the Main method, including local variable information. You will use the address of the object to analyze the following code:

```
0:000> !clrstack -a
OS Thread Id: 0x139c (0)
Child SP IP    Call Site
002ced64 003f0110 CH_05.Book.Print()*** WARNING: Unable to verify checksum for CH_05.exe
 [J:\Book\C# Deconstructed\SourceCode\Chapters\CH_05\Program.cs @ 17]
    PARAMETERS:
        this (<CLR reg>) = 0x01f7b684

002ced68 003f00b4 CH_05.Program.Main(System.String[]) [J:\Book\C# Deconstructed\SourceCode\Chapters\
CH_05\Program.cs @ 10]
    PARAMETERS:
        args (0x002ced70) = 0x01f7b674
    LOCALS:
        0x002ced6c = 0x01f7b684

002cefac 586e21db [GCFrame: 002cefac]
```

Let's examine the memory contents of the object located at 0x0163b77c, which demonstrate how the CLR lays out an object in memory:

```
0:000> dc 0x01f7b684-100
01f7b584  ffffffff 01f7b300 00000000 011ecf05   ...............
01f7b594  ffffffff 01f7b318 00000000 0215472d   ............-G..
01f7b5a4  ffffffff 00000000 00000000 00000000   ...............
01f7b5b4  00000000 00000000 00000000 00000000   ...............
01f7b5c4  00000000 00000000 00000000 00000000   ...............
01f7b5d4  00000000 00000000 00000000 00000000   ...............
01f7b5e4  00000000 00000000 00000000 00000000   ...............
01f7b5f4  00000000 00000000 00000000 00000000   ...............
```

The output shows the header of the object, which has a few elements, including Syncblk and TypeHandle, and instance fields.

You can use the !dumpobject (do) command to present the object structure in more user-friendly fashion:

```
0:000> !do 0x01f7b684
Name:        CH_05.Book
MethodTable: 00343880
EEClass:     00341480
Size:        12(0xc) bytes
File:        J:\Book\C# Deconstructed\SourceCode\Chapters\CH_05\bin\Debug\CH_05.exe
Fields:
None
```

Now, let's look at the method table information:

```
0:000> !dumpmt -MD 00343880
EEClass:       00341480
Module:        00342e9c
Name:          CH_05.Book
mdToken:       02000003
File:          J:\Book\C# Deconstructed\SourceCode\Chapters\CH_05\bin\Debug\CH_05.exe
BaseSize:      0xc
ComponentSize: 0x0
Slots in VTable: 6
Number of IFaces in IFaceMap: 0
----------------------------------------
MethodDesc Table
   Entry MethodDesc      JIT Name
571ea7e0    56fc4934    PreJIT System.Object.ToString()
571ee2e0    56fc493c    PreJIT System.Object.Equals(System.Object)
571ee1f0    56fc495c    PreJIT System.Object.GetHashCode()
57271600    56fc4970    PreJIT System.Object.Finalize()
003f00d0    00343878      JIT CH_05.Book..ctor()
003f0110    0034386c      JIT CH_05.Book.Print()
```

Let's examine as well the desc method:

```
0:000> !dumpmd 0034386c
Method Name:  CH_05.Book.Print()
Class:        00341480
MethodTable:  00343880
mdToken:      06000003
Module:       00342e9c
IsJitted:     yes
CodeAddr:     003f0110
Transparency: Critical
```

Garbage Collection

When you create an instance of a type in .NET, such as a reference type, using a new keyword, the CLR takes care of the rest. For example, the CLR will instantiate the type onto the heap, allocate extra memory as needed, and deallocate the memory when you finish with that object. The CLR carries out this memory reclaim process using the GC. The GC maintains information about object usage and uses this information to make memory management decisions, such as where in the memory to locate a newly created object, when to relocate an object, and when an object is no longer to be in use or accessible.

In .NET automatic memory cleanup is achieved using the GC algorithm. This algorithm looks for an allocated object on the heap and tries to determine if that object is being referenced by anything; if it is not, the GC will allocate it for collection or to the cleanup cycle. There are several possible sources of these references:

- Global or static object references

- CPU registers

- Object finalization references

- Interoperability references (.NET objects passed to Component Object Model [COM]/API calls)

- Stack references

The GC needs to traverse a number of objects to determine whether they can be collected for cleanup. The CLR uses the concept of longevity of the object in memory. For instance, when the object is in use for a long time, it is less likely to lose the reference, whereas a newly created object is more likely to be cleaned up.

In GC, three generations of object groups are used:

- Generation 0

- Generation 1

- Generation 2

Generation 0

Generation 0 (Gen 0) is the youngest group, and it contains short-lived objects. An example of a short-lived object is a temporary variable. GC occurs most frequently in this generation. Newly allocated objects form a new generation of objects and are implicitly Gen 0 collections, unless they are large objects, in which case they go on the LOH in a Gen 2 collection. Most objects are reclaimed for GC in Gen 0 and do not survive to the next generation.

Generation 1

Gen 1 contains short-lived objects and serves as a buffer between short-lived objects and long-lived objects.

Generation 2

Gen 2 contains long-lived objects. An example of a long-lived object is a server application that contains static data that are live for the duration of the process.

The life of an object starts in Gen 0. If the objects in Gen 0 survive, the GC promotes them to Gen 1, and likewise for the promotion of Gen 1 objects to Gen 2. The objects in Gen 2 stay in Gen 2. Gen 0 objects are collected frequently, so short-lived objects are quickly removed. Gen 1 objects are collected less frequently, and Gen 2 objects, even less frequently. Thus, the longer an object lives, the longer it takes to remove from memory once it has lost all references. When Gen 1 objects are collected, the GC gathers Gen 0 objects as well. In addition, when Gen 2 objects are collected, those in Gen 1 and Gen 0 are also collected. As a result, higher-generation collections are more expensive.

GC cleanup consists of three phases:

- *Marking phase*: The GC finds and creates a list of all live objects.

- *Relocating phase*: The GC updates the references to the objects that will be compacted.

- *Compacting phase*: The GC reclaims the space occupied by the dead objects and compacts the surviving objects; the compacting phase moves objects that have survived the GC toward the older end of the segment.

Gen 2 collections can occupy multiple segments; objects that are promoted to Gen 2 can be moved to an older segment. Both Gen 1 and Gen 2 survivors can be moved to a different segment, because they are promoted to Gen 2. The LOH is not compacted, as this would increase memory usage to an unacceptable length of time.

Conclusion

In Chapters 4 and 5, you saw how the OS manages the use of physical memory and the layout of the application program by the CLR. You also explored further the concept of the process, a mechanism that splits different sets of functionality into their own boundaries. The OS takes care of this process, using data structure and specification; the OS allows the process to have its own private virtual address space, thereby ensuring that the process runs in an isolated boundary. The OS treats the CLR is like a process. So, to understand how the CLR execution model and JIT compiler work, you need to know how the OS handles the CLR, forexample, its loading process, memory layout for the application code, metadata, and resources. In the next chapter, you will examine the CLR execution model. In addition, you will study the CLR bootstrapping process and the different components of the CLR.

Further Reading

Farrell, C., & Harrison, N. (2011). *Under the Hood of. NET Memory Management*. Simple Talk Pub..

Hewardt, Mario. *Advanced .NET Debugging*. Upper Saddle River, NJ: Addison-Wesley, 2010.

Hewardt, Mario, and Daniel Pravat. *Advanced Windows Debugging*. Upper Saddle River, NJ: Addison-Wesley, 2008.

Jacob, Bruce, Spencer W. Ng, and David T. Wang. *Memory Systems: Cache, DRAM, Disk*. Burlington, MA: Morgan Kaufmann, 2010.

Juola, Patrick. *Principles of Computer Organization and Assembly Language*. Upper Saddle River, NJ: Prentice Hall, 2007.

Lidin, Serge. *Inside Microsoft .NET IL Assembler*. Redmond, WA: Microsoft.

McDougall, Richard, and Jim Mauro. *Solaris Internals: Solaris 10 and OpenSolaris Kernel Architecture*. Upper Saddle River, NJ: Prentice Hall, 2006.

Pratschner, Steven. *Customizing the Microsoft .NET Framework Common Language Runtime*. Edited by Kathleen Atkins. Redmond, WA: Microsoft, 2009.

CHAPTER 6

■ ■ ■

CLR Execution Model

The CLR is a virtual execution environment that is used to execute and manage managed code execution. In .NET the code that provides information such as metadata to describe the method, property, class, and other elements of a type; walks through the stack; manages and handles exceptions; and furnishes security over the code to allow the CLI to offer a set of core services is referred to as managed code. As discussed previously, the CLR is implemented by the CLI and CTS and supplies services, including automatic memory management, using GC (see Chapter 1); metadata to describe the types and control type discovery, loading, and layout; analysis of managed libraries and programs (see Chapter 3); a robust exception management subsystem to enable programs to communicate and respond to failures in structured ways; native and legacy code interoperability; JIT compilation of managed code into native code; and a sophisticated security infrastructure.

In this chapter, you will learn about the CLR, including bootstrapping of the CLR and class loading. This will help advance your understanding of how the CLR manages managed code execution and manages virtual address space to define AppDomain, Stack, Heap; and so on to create the execution environment, verification that is performed while compiling the IL code at JIT compile time.

Overview of the CLR

The CLR is a standard Windows process that acts as a virtual execution environment for the .NET languages. The CLR uses OS services to facilitate the loading, compilation, and execution of an assembly. The CLR serves as an execution abstraction for the .NET languages. To achieve this, it uses a set of DLLs, which acts as a middle layer between the OS and the application program. The CLR itself is a collection of DLLs, and these DLLs work together to define the virtual execution environment. The DLLs are

- mscoree.dll
- clr.dll
- mscorsvr.dll or mscorwks.dll
- And others

When we say that the CLR executes managed code, what we mean is that the managed code does not execute directly, via the CPU itself. To be execute by the CPU, however, the application program does not need to implement any special mechanisms; the CLR handles the execution, using the OS services. The CLR maintains the activation frame on method invocation to maintain the state of method call, handle the context switch, manage the object life cycle at runtime, and so on. If you ever have the opportunity to examine native code generated by the JIT compiler, you will find that much of it references the aforementioned DLLs (e.g., CLR.DLL). These DLLs work, along with the application code, to offer the services mentioned earlier.

Let's take a look at the following C# program, which is being compiled using the C# compiler (csc.exe) and debugged with WinDbg:

```csharp
using System;

namespace CH_06
{
    class Program
    {
        static void Main(string[] args)
        {
            ClassTest ct = new ClassTest();
            ct.Print();
        }
    }

    public class ClassTest
    {
        public void Print()
        {
            Console.WriteLine(ToString());
        }
    }
}
```

Once this application is compiled into an assembly (CH_06.exe), using csc.exe, you load the assembly into WinDbg to start debugging. You will be using the following WinDbg command to initialize the debugging session:

```
0:000> sxe ld clrjit
0:000> g
0:000> .loadby sos clr
0:000> .load C:\Windows\Microsoft.NET\Framework\v4.0.30319\sos.dll
```

Now, you set a few breakpoints, as shown:

```
0:000> !bpmd CH_06.exe CH_06.ClassTest.Print
Found 1 methods in module 00342e9c...
Adding pending breakpoints...

0:000> !bpmd CH_06.exe CH_06.Program.Main
Found 1 methods in module 00342e9c...
MethodDesc = 00343800
Adding pending breakpoints...

0:000>g

0:000> !name2ee CH_06.exe CH_06.Program.Main
Module:         00142e9c
Assembly:       CH_06.exe
Token:          06000001
MethodDesc:     00143800
Name:           CH_06.Program.Main(System.String[])
JITTED Code Address: 003d0070
```

The !u command of WinDbg is used with the method description address to display an annotated disassembly of the managed method:

```
0:000> !u 003d0070
Normal JIT generated code
CH_06.Program.Main(System.String[])
Begin 003d0070, size 50
J:\Book\C# Deconstructed\SourceCode\Chapters\CH_06\Program.cs @ 8:
>>> 003c0070 55              push    ebp
003c0071 8bec               mov     ebp,esp
003c0073 83ec0c             sub     esp,0Ch
003c0076 894dfc             mov     dword ptr [ebp-4],ecx
003c0079 833d3c31340000     cmp     dword ptr ds:[34313Ch],0
003c0080 7405               je      003c0087
003c0082 e8c85a6953         call    clr!JIT_DbgIsJustMyCode (53a55b4f)
003c0087 33d2               xor     edx,edx
003c0089 8955f8             mov     dword ptr [ebp-8],edx
003c008c 90                 nop

J:\Book\C# Deconstructed\SourceCode\Chapters\CH_06\Program.cs @ 9:
003c008d b980383400         mov     ecx,343880h (MT: CH_06.ClassTest)
003c0092 e8891ff7ff         call    00332020 (JitHelp: CORINFO_HELP_NEWSFAST)
003c0097 8945f4             mov     dword ptr [ebp-0Ch],eax
003c009a 8b4df4             mov     ecx,dword ptr [ebp-0Ch]
003c009d ff15ac383400       call    dword ptr ds:[3438ACh] (CH_06.ClassTest..ctor(), mdToken: 06000004)
003c00a3 8b45f4             mov     eax,dword ptr [ebp-0Ch]
003c00a6 8945f8             mov     dword ptr [ebp-8],eax

J:\Book\C# Deconstructed\SourceCode\Chapters\CH_06\Program.cs @ 10:
003c00a9 8b4df8             mov     ecx,dword ptr [ebp-8]
003c00ac 3909               cmp     dword ptr [ecx],ecx
003c00ae ff1574383400       call    dword ptr ds:[343874h] (CH_06.ClassTest.Print(), mdToken: 06000003)
003c00b4 90                 nop

J:\Book\C# Deconstructed\SourceCode\Chapters\CH_06\Program.cs @ 11:
003c00b5 90                 nop
003c00b6 8be5               mov     esp,ebp
003c00b8 5d                 pop     ebp
003c00b9 c3                 ret
```

When you write an application program using one of the .NET languages, you probably never think to use methods such as clr!JIT_DbgIsJustMyCode from your application program. The CLR is responsible for doing this. Figure 6-1 demonstrates the core components of the CLR, which include the assembly, class loader, and JIT compiler as well as other services, such as the GC and security.

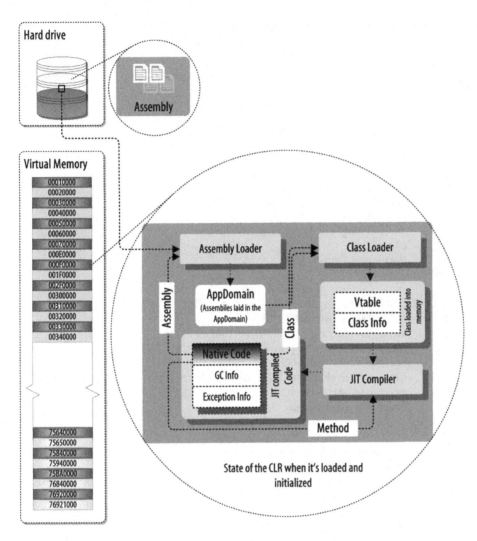

Figure 6-1. *Overview of the CLR execution model*

To load the assemblies, the CLR is using the assembly loader component. The assembly-loading process can also be used by the method that is currently executing. Let's say, for example, a method is executing, and during its execution, there is a reference to a functionality that is not in the running assembly, but resides in a different assembly. As it is not yet loaded into memory, there is no chance of obtaining that method's native code. You must therefore load that assembly into the memory.

Initially, the assembly needs to be loaded into memory by the assembly loader. Once it has been loaded into memory, the assembly has to locate the appropriate class to find the relevant method for which it has been loaded. The class loader component of the CLR will load the class and lay out the metadata in memory. After loading the class, the next step is to perform a JIT compilation.

The JIT compiler is used to compile any method defined in any type from IL code into the native code. If the method has not yet been compiled into the native code, the JIT compiler will compile it; if it has already been compiled, the CLR will use that compiled native code to execute. While the native code is executing, if it references a member that is in a different class but that is in an assembly that has already been loaded, the CLR will invoke the class loader to create the appropriate data structures, such as MethodTable, and other, related metadata for use by the calling method.

The CLR offers another function that enforces security by stopping the execution of illegal code—code that generates an invalid address and jumps to it, thereby bypassing the CLR's normal execution flow.

The CLR executes native code derived from a verified assembly, such as one generated by a CLI-compliant compiler. There are a couple of ways for the CLR to make sure that an assembly has been verified (as described in Partition I of the ECMA C# standard, which is available on the ECMA web site [http://www.ecma-international.org/publications/standards/Ecma-335.htm]):

- The assembly was downloaded from a trusted source, and it is assured not to have been tampered with.

- The EE runs its own verification tool on the assembly to ensure that it is type safe.

So far, you have seen how the CLR handles the execution of your code. In the following section, you will view an example demonstrating the execution model used in the CLR. Then, you will explore the assembly loader, class loader, JIT compiler, and method state, while the CLR executes your code in detail.

The C# Program and the CLR

As mentioned earlier, a .NET application uses two types of compiler, from compilation to execution phase. The front-end compiler (e.g., csc.exe, in C# language) compiles the C# source code into the IL code and generates metadata (to define the IL code). The back-end compiler is the JIT compiler, which compiles the IL code into native code.

Figure 6-2 shows that the C# source code is compiled by the C# compiler to generate the assembly. This assembly contains IL code that is equivalent to C# code and metadata to define the types used in the IL code and PE and CLR header information (see Chapter 3) to define the assembly.

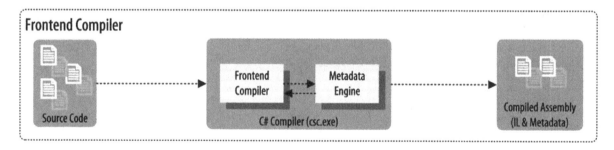

Figure 6-2. C# compilation

The following C# program demonstrates how the C# compiler compiles your application code into an assembly and how the CLR loads the assembly into memory and manages the execution of that assembly at runtime. By providing services, such as class loading, verification, JIT compilation, and code management, the CLR creates an environment for code execution, the VES.

```
using System;

namespace CH_06
{
    class Program
    {
        static void Main(string[] args)
        {
            Console.WriteLine(Math.PI);
        }
    }
}
```

When this application is compiled into an assembly (CH_06.exe), using csc.exe, the CLR's metadata engine enables the source code compiler to place metadata in the PE file, along with the generated IL code.

Next, you use the dumpbin.exe tool with the /HEADER flag, as shown:

```
dumpbin /HEADERS CH_06.exe
```

This will generate the following output:

```
Microsoft (R) COFF/PE Dumper Version 10.00.40219.01
Copyright (C) Microsoft Corporation.  All rights reserved.

Dump of file Program.exe

PE signature found

File Type: EXECUTABLE IMAGE

FILE HEADER VALUES
             14C machine (x86)
               3 number of sections
        530AB43E time date stamp Mon Feb 24 13:53:50 2014
               0 file pointer to symbol table
               0 number of symbols
              E0 size of optional header
             102 characteristics
                    Executable
                    32 bit word machine

OPTIONAL HEADER VALUES
             10B magic # (PE32)
            8.00 linker version
             400 size of code
             800 size of initialized data
               0 size of uninitialized data
            23DE entry point (004023DE)
            2000 base of code
            4000 base of data
          400000 image base (00400000 to 00407FFF)
```

```
          2000 section alignment
           200 file alignment
          4.00 operating system version
          0.00 image version
          4.00 subsystem version
             0 Win32 version
          8000 size of image
           200 size of headers
             0 checksum
             3 subsystem (Windows CUI)
          8540 DLL characteristics
                   Dynamic base
                   NX compatible
                   No structured exception handler
                   Terminal Server Aware
        100000 size of stack reserve
          1000 size of stack commit
        100000 size of heap reserve
          1000 size of heap commit
             0 loader flags
            10 number of directories
             0 [        0] RVA [size] of Export Directory
          2384 [       57] RVA [size] of Import Directory
          4000 [      4D8] RVA [size] of Resource Directory
             0 [        0] RVA [size] of Exception Directory
             0 [        0] RVA [size] of Certificates Directory
          6000 [        C] RVA [size] of Base Relocation Directory
             0 [        0] RVA [size] of Debug Directory
             0 [        0] RVA [size] of Architecture Directory
             0 [        0] RVA [size] of Global Pointer Directory
             0 [        0] RVA [size] of Thread Storage Directory
             0 [        0] RVA [size] of Load Configuration Directory
             0 [        0] RVA [size] of Bound Import Directory
          2000 [        8] RVA [size] of Import Address Table Directory
             0 [        0] RVA [size] of Delay Import Directory
          2008 [       48] RVA [size] of COM Descriptor Directory
             0 [        0] RVA [size] of Reserved Directory

SECTION HEADER #1
   .text name
     3E4 virtual size
    2000 virtual address (00402000 to 004023E3)
     400 size of raw data
     200 file pointer to raw data (00000200 to 000005FF)
       0 file pointer to relocation table
       0 file pointer to line numbers
       0 number of relocations
       0 number of line numbers
60000020 flags
         Code
         Execute Read
```

117

SECTION HEADER #2
    .rsrc name
      4D8 virtual size
     4000 virtual address (00404000 to 004044D7)
      600 size of raw data
      600 file pointer to raw data (00000600 to 00000BFF)
        0 file pointer to relocation table
        0 file pointer to line numbers
        0 number of relocations
        0 number of line numbers
 40000040 flags
          Initialized Data
          Read Only

SECTION HEADER #3
    .reloc name
        C virtual size
     6000 virtual address (00406000 to 0040600B)
      200 size of raw data
      C00 file pointer to raw data (00000C00 to 00000DFF)
        0 file pointer to relocation table
        0 file pointer to line numbers
        0 number of relocations
        0 number of line numbers
 42000040 flags
          Initialized Data
          Discardable
          Read Only

    Summary

        2000 .reloc
        2000 .rsrc
        2000 .text

As you can see, the IL code is compiled by the C# front-end compiler, and it will be further compiled by the JIT compiler at runtime to generate the native code. This compiled native code will later be executed by the execution engine of the CLR, as illustrated in Figure 6-3.

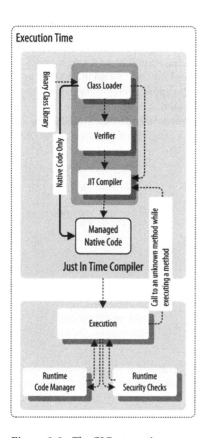

Figure 6-3. *The CLR at runtime*

In .NET the source code is compiled into IL code, along with the metadata, which later loads, verifies, and JIT compiles to produce the native code on the fly, using the runtime compiler JIT. The metadata provide enough information to the CLR for registration, debugging, memory management, and security. It is for this reason that this code is also referred to as managed code. The assembly loader loads an assembly, and the class loader component loads required classes from the assembly as well as related classes from .NET Framework libraries, as indicated in the figure.

The JIT compilation at runtime can be omitted, using the precompilation process supported by the CLR. In this process, IL code is precompiled into the native code, using a tool such as ngen.exe, before the containing assembly is executed, to avoid JIT compilation while the assembly is executed by the CLR.

As discussed in Chapter 1, the CLR is a Windows process, and it controls the execution of the managed code. The CLR itself cannot be loaded into memory to work as the execution environment; it needs to be triggered to load and start as a process. In this case, a piece of code, known as bootstrapper, which is embedded in the application program during compilation, is used to trigger the CLR to initialize and load into memory. Once the CLR has been loaded, it is in charge of the application program for which it's being loaded, and it will take care of execution of that application program.

Bootstrapping is the mechanism used for loading the CLR. In the next section, I will discuss the CLR bootstrapping process in detail.

CLR Bootstrapping

The CLR is made up of a number of DLLs. It does not do anything unless they are being loaded by an application as a host for them. The CLR works as the mediator between the application program and the OS. To load these DLLs to initialize the execution environment and start executing the application program, the application program needs to tell the Windows loader that this is a .NET application and that the CLR has to be loaded.

The bootstrapping process of the CLR is triggered by a piece of code. This thin piece of code, embedded in the assembly, triggers the execution process of the application program. Figure 6-4 gives a high-level overview of the CLR bootstrapping process.

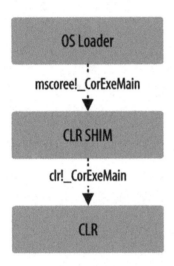

Figure 6-4. *CLR bootstrapping*

The bootstrapper of an executable simply uses a method call to the _CorExeMain method, located in mscoree.dll. If you examine any C# assembly, and look for the mscoree.dll import table, you will find a reference to the _CorExeMain method. You use the dumpbin tool, from the Visual Studio command prompt, to find the Imports section of mscoree.dll, using this command:

```
dumpbin /IMPORTS "J:\Book\C# Deconstructed\SourceCode\Chapters\CH_06\bin\Debug\CH_06.exe"
```

It shows the following output:

```
Microsoft (R) COFF/PE Dumper Version 10.00.30319.01
Copyright (C) Microsoft Corporation.  All rights reserved.

Dump of file J:\Book\C# Deconstructed\SourceCode\Chapters\CH_06\bin\Debug\CH_06.
exe

File Type: EXECUTABLE IMAGE
```

Section contains the following imports:

```
mscoree.dll
              402000 Import Address Table
              4026F0 Import Name Table
                   0 time date stamp
                   0 Index of first forwarder reference

                   0 _CorExeMain
```

Summary

```
        2000 .reloc
        2000 .rsrc
        2000 .text
```

The _CorExeMain method, from mscoree.dll, contains code that has forwarded a call to the mscoree.dll!_CorDllMain method. Let's take a look at the disassembled version of the _CorExeMain method, which displays how the CLR shim process is triggered:

```
0:000> u mscoree!_CorExeMain_Exported
mscoree!_CorExeMain_Exported:
79004ddb 8bff            mov      edi,edi
79004ddd 56              push     esi
79004dde e80c2f0000      call     mscoree!ShellShim__CorExeMain (79007cef)
79004de3 6a00            push     0
79004de5 8bf0            mov      esi,eax
79004de7 e84bc4ffff      call     mscoree!GetShimImpl (79001237)
79004dec e93a800000      jmp      mscoree!_CorExeMain_Exported+0x11 (7900ce2b)
                                  mscoree!_imp_load__RegOpenKeyExW:
79004df1 b82c100479      mov      eax,offset mscoree!_imp__RegOpenKeyExW (7904102c)
```

The shim is responsible for selecting either the workstation or the server build of the CLR, which is found in mscorwks.dll and mscorsvr.dll. The shim process is triggered by the MSCOREE!ShellShim__CorExeMain method, which can be explored by examining the stack trace of the CLR loading. You can use the following program to explore how the CLR is triggered:

```
using System;

namespace CH_06
{
    class Program
    {
        static void Main(string[] args){}
    }
}
```

Once this application is compiled into an assembly (CH_06.exe), using csc.exe, you load this assembly into WinDbg to start debugging. You will be using these commands to initialize the debugging session:

```
0:000> sxe ld clrjit
0:000> g
0:000> .loadby sos clr
0:000> .load C:\Windows\Microsoft.NET\Framework\v4.0.30319\sos.dll
```

Now, you can use ~0 kn or !eestack -short, as both give the same result:

```
0:000> !eestack -short
--------------------------------------------
Thread   0
Current frame: ntdll!KiFastSystemCallRet
ChildEBP RetAddr  Caller, Callee
/* removed*/
002ffa14 71767f16 MSCOREE!ShellShim__CorExeMain+0x99
002ffa24 71764de3 MSCOREE!_CorExeMain_Exported+0x8, calling MSCOREE!ShellShim__CorExeMain
002ffa2c 76a21174 KERNEL32!BaseThreadInitThunk+0xe
002ffa38 774eb3f5 ntdll!__RtlUserThreadStart+0x70
002ffa78 774eb3c8 ntdll!_RtlUserThreadStart+0x1b, calling ntdll!__RtlUserThreadStart
--------------------------------------------
Thread   2
```

–SHORT PARAMETER

The -short parameter limits the output to the following kinds of threads:

- Threads that have taken a lock

- Threads that have been stalled to allow a garbage collection

- Threads that are currently in managed code

The shim is a block of code that accepts a version number and other startup parameters from the host and starts the CLR. Only one version of the shim exists on a given machine, and that version is installed on the machine's default search path (currently %windir%\system32). During the shim process the shim will call the mscoreei!_CorExeMain method to ascertain the entry point of the assembly for starting the execution. Typically, the entry point is the Main method for the executable assembly:

```
0:000> !u mscoree!ShellShim__CorExeMain
Unmanaged code
71767cef 8bff          mov      edi,edi
71767cf1 55            push     ebp
71767cf2 8bec          mov      ebp,esp
71767cf4 51            push     ecx
71767cf5 8365fc00      and      dword ptr [ebp-4],0
71767cf9 8d45fc        lea      eax,[ebp-4]
71767cfc 50            push     eax
71767cfd e83595ffff    call     MSCOREE!GetShimImpl (71761237)
71767d02 83f801        cmp      eax,1
71767d05 0f84164c0000  je       MSCOREE!ShellShim__CorExeMain+0x18 (7176c921)
```

```
0:000> !u MSCOREE!ShellShim__CorExeMain+0x18
Unmanaged code
71767d07 16            push    ss
71767d08 4c            dec     esp
71767d09 0000          add     byte ptr [eax],al
71767d0b 83f803        cmp     eax,3
71767d0e 0f84243a0000  je      MSCOREE!ShellShim__CorExeMain+0x24 (7176b738)
71767d14 a194107a71    mov     eax,dword ptr [MSCOREE!g_bShimImplDllUninitialized (717a1094)]
71767d19 85c0          test    eax,eax
71767d1b 0f84074c0000  je      MSCOREE!ShellShim__CorExeMain+0x34 (7176c928)
71767d21 e9fb4b0000    jmp     MSCOREE!ShellShim__CorExeMain+0x18 (7176c921)
71767d26 85d2          test    edx,edx
```

The shim is kept as small and straightforward as possible to ensure its compatibility with future versions of the CLR. The startup shim ties the multiple versions of the CLR together. Specifically, the shim tracks which versions are installed and is capable of finding the location on disk of a specific version of the CLR. Because of its role as arbitrator, the shim is not installed side by side. Each machine has only one copy of mscoree.dll installed on %windir%\system32:

```
0:000> !address /f:IMAGE
....
Image       [MSCOREE; "C:\Windows\SYSTEM32\MSCOREE.DLL"]
721c1000 72201000    40000 MEM_IMAGE    MEM_COMMIT   PAGE_EXECUTE_READ   Image   [MSCOREE; "C:\Windows\
                                                                                 SYSTEM32\MSCOREE.DLL"]
72201000 72205000     4000 MEM_IMAGE    MEM_COMMIT   PAGE_READWRITE      Image   [MSCOREE; "C:\Windows\
                                                                                 SYSTEM32\MSCOREE.DLL"]
72205000 7220a000     5000 MEM_IMAGE    MEM_COMMIT   PAGE_READONLY       Image   [MSCOREE; "C:\Windows\
                                                                                 SYSTEM32\MSCOREE.DLL"]
.....
```

Requests to load the CLR come through the startup shim, which then directs each request to the version of the CLR indicated. The shim decides where to look for these DLLs and which flavor to load based on a number of factors, including registry settings and whether the user is on a uni- or multiprocessor machine. From there, other DLLs are loaded as needed to execute the managed code. For instance, mscorjit.dll is used to compile IL to JIT (in the case of non-native image generator [NGen] assemblies). The shim then calls the _CorExeMain method to determine the entry point and start loading, as shown in the disassembled code of mscoree!ShellShim__CorExeMain+0x18 (7900c921):

```
*>,&DoTheRelease<ICLRRuntimeInfo>,2>,0,&CompareDefault<ICLRRuntimeInfo *>,2>+0x30, calling
  mscoreei!_EH_epilog3
0030fbec 5c66af00 clr!_CorExeMain+0x4e, calling clr!_CorExeMainInternal
0030fc24 716755ab mscoreei!_CorExeMain+0x38
0030fc30 716e7f16 MSCOREE!ShellShim__CorExeMain+0x99
0030fc40 716e4de3 MSCOREE!_CorExeMain_Exported+0x8, calling MSCOREE!ShellShim__CorExeMain
```

The CLR is now in charge, and it will start reading the executable to read the manifest, metadata, and IL code that reside in the assembly and begin processing it from the managed entry point. As you have already seen, the assembly that is trying to be executed contains the IL code, which is never executed by the processor, as it is stored as data.

CLR Address Space

Before considering the CLR execution model, let's quickly look at the address space allocation that occurs when the CLR is loaded into memory. The address space is a range of virtual memory addresses that allow metadata, types, and IL or native code mapped to it and other external assemblies to be mapped. If you examine the following disassembled code of the mscoree!ShellShim__CorExeMain+0x18 (7900c921)method, you will see that it calls mscoree!_imp__GetProcAddress to initialize the address space:

```
7900c92e 8b3518100079    mov     esi,dword ptr [mscoree!_imp__GetProcAddress (79001018)]
```

Now, let's perform a small experiment here, using the following C# program to explore address space:

```csharp
using System;

namespace CH_06
{
    class Program
    {
        static void Main(string[] args) { }
    }
}
```

Once this application is compiled into an assembly (CH_06.exe), using csc.exe, you load this assembly into WinDbg to start debugging. Use the following WinDbg command to initialize the debugging session:

```
0:000> sxe ld clrjit
0:000> g
0:000> .loadby sos clr
0:000> .load C:\Windows\Microsoft.NET\Framework\v4.0.30319\sos.dll
```

Before debugging the loaded assembly, set a breakpoint, using !bpmd at the Main method of this assembly, and then continue with the execution, using g. Once the breakpoint, is hit, you study the MethodTable of the Program class to determine the JIT status of the Main method, which is the entry point of this assembly:

```
0:000> !dumpmt -MD 00313804
EEClass:        003113ec
Module:         00312e9c
Name:           CH_06.Program
mdToken:        02000002
File:           J:\Book\C# Deconstructed\SourceCode\Chapters\CH_06\bin\Debug\CH_06.exe
BaseSize:       0xc
ComponentSize:  0x0
Slots in VTable: 6
Number of IFaces in IFaceMap: 0
--------------------------------------
MethodDesc Table
   Entry MethodDesc      JIT Name
55faa7e0    55d84934   PreJIT System.Object.ToString()
55fae2e0    55d8493c   PreJIT System.Object.Equals(System.Object)
55fae1f0    55d8495c   PreJIT System.Object.GetHashCode()
56031600    55d84970   PreJIT System.Object.Finalize()
0031c015    003137fc     NONE CH_06.Program..ctor()
00500070    003137f0      JIT CH_06.Program.Main(System.String[])
```

The output demonstrates that the Main method has not yet been JIT compiled, but the CLR creates the appropriate address space for allocating the different abstract memory regions.

Next, you examine the address space, using the WindDg tool to see how the CLR allocates address space to initialize its virtual memory abstraction concept, such as AppDomain, Stack, or Heap. You will use the !address command with different flags, such as summary, in the WinDbg tool to get the address space details:

```
0:000> !address -summary
```

--- Usage Summary ----------------	RgnCount	----------- Total Size --------	%ofBusy	%ofTotal
Free	48	7a498000 (1.911 Gb)		95.54%
<unknown>	32	2105000 (33.020 Mb)	36.15%	1.61%
Image	139	1ee0000 (30.875 Mb)	33.80%	1.51%
MappedFile	12	13dc000 (19.859 Mb)	21.74%	0.97%
Stack	17	400000 (4.000 Mb)	4.38%	0.20%
Heap	20	260000 (2.375 Mb)	2.60%	0.12%
Other	9	132000 (1.195 Mb)	1.31%	0.06%
TEB	4	4000 (16.000 kb)	0.02%	0.00%
PEB	1	1000 (4.000 kb)	0.00%	0.00%

This shows the overall view of the different memory regions, such as Stack, Heap, and MappedFile, allocated by the CLR. The !address command has different options that can be used to see the different regions of memory. You will use the f flag with STACK, HEAP, PAGEHEAP, IMAGE, FILEMap, PEB, and TEB options to see how the address space has been divided into these regions:

```
0:000> !address /f:STACK
```

BaseAddr	EndAddr+1	RgnSize	Type	State	Protect	Usage
80000	81000	1000	MEM_PRIVATE	MEM_RESERVE		Stack [~0; 88c.fc8]
81000	179000	f8000	MEM_PRIVATE	MEM_COMMIT	PAGE_READWRITE	Stack [~0; 88c.fc8]
179000	17b000	2000	MEM_PRIVATE	MEM_COMMIT	PAGE_READWRITE|PAGE_GUARD	Stack [~0; 88c.fc8]
17b000	180000	5000	MEM_PRIVATE	MEM_COMMIT	PAGE_READWRITE	Stack [~0; 88c.fc8]
1530000	1531000	1000	MEM_PRIVATE	MEM_RESERVE		Stack [~1; 88c.ec4]
1531000	162d000	fc000	MEM_PRIVATE	MEM_COMMIT	PAGE_READWRITE	Stack [~1; 88c.ec4]
162d000	162f000	2000	MEM_PRIVATE	MEM_COMMIT	PAGE_READWRITE|PAGE_GUARD	Stack [~1; 88c.ec4]
162f000	1630000	1000	MEM_PRIVATE	MEM_COMMIT	PAGE_READWRITE	Stack [~1; 88c.ec4]
36b0000	36b1000	1000	MEM_PRIVATE	MEM_RESERVE		Stack [~2; 88c.640]
36b1000	36b2000	1000	MEM_PRIVATE	MEM_COMMIT	PAGE_READWRITE	Stack [~2; 88c.640]
36b2000	36b4000	2000	MEM_PRIVATE	MEM_COMMIT	PAGE_READWRITE|PAGE_GUARD	Stack [~2; 88c.640]
36b4000	37ac000	f8000	MEM_PRIVATE	MEM_COMMIT	PAGE_READWRITE	Stack [~2; 88c.640]
37ac000	37ae000	2000	MEM_PRIVATE	MEM_COMMIT	PAGE_READWRITE|PAGE_GUARD	Stack [~2; 88c.640]
37ae000	37b0000	2000	MEM_PRIVATE	MEM_COMMIT	PAGE_READWRITE	Stack [~2; 88c.640]
3b00000	3bfd000	fd000	MEM_PRIVATE	MEM_RESERVE		Stack [~3; 88c.f80]
3bfd000	3bff000	2000	MEM_PRIVATE	MEM_COMMIT	PAGE_READWRITE|PAGE_GUARD	Stack [~3; 88c.f80]
3bff000	3c00000	1000	MEM_PRIVATE	MEM_COMMIT	PAGE_READWRITE	Stack [~3; 88c.f80]

```
0:000> !address /f:HEAP
```

BaseAddr	EndAddr+1	RgnSize	Type	State	Protect	Usage
10000	20000	10000	MEM_MAPPED	MEM_COMMIT	PAGE_READWRITE	Heap [ID: 1; Handle: 00010000; Type: Segment]
20000	30000	10000	MEM_MAPPED	MEM_COMMIT	PAGE_READWRITE	Heap [ID: 2; Handle: 00020000; Type: Segment]
210000	213000	3000	MEM_PRIVATE	MEM_COMMIT	PAGE_READWRITE	Heap [ID: 5; Handle: 00210000; Type: Segment]
213000	220000	d000	MEM_PRIVATE	MEM_RESERVE		Heap [ID: 5; Handle: 00210000; Type: Segment]
220000	221000	1000	MEM_PRIVATE	MEM_COMMIT	PAGE_EXECUTE_READWRITE	Heap [ID: 7; Handle: 00220000; Type: Segment]
221000	260000	3f000	MEM_PRIVATE	MEM_RESERVE		Heap [ID: 7; Handle: 00220000; Type: Segment]
350000	353000	3000	MEM_PRIVATE	MEM_COMMIT	PAGE_READWRITE	Heap [ID: 3; Handle: 00350000; Type: Segment]
353000	360000	d000	MEM_PRIVATE	MEM_RESERVE		Heap [ID: 3; Handle: 00350000; Type: Segment]
3e0000	3e3000	3000	MEM_PRIVATE	MEM_COMMIT	PAGE_READWRITE	Heap [ID: 8; Handle: 003e0000; Type: Segment]
3e3000	3f0000	d000	MEM_PRIVATE	MEM_RESERVE		Heap [ID: 8; Handle: 003e0000; Type: Segment]
430000	497000	67000	MEM_PRIVATE	MEM_COMMIT	PAGE_READWRITE	Heap [ID: 0; Handle: 00430000; Type: Segment]
497000	530000	99000	MEM_PRIVATE	MEM_RESERVE		Heap [ID: 0; Handle: 00430000; Type: Segment]
680000	683000	3000	MEM_PRIVATE	MEM_COMMIT	PAGE_READWRITE	Heap [ID: 6; Handle: 00680000; Type: Segment]
683000	690000	d000	MEM_PRIVATE	MEM_RESERVE		Heap [ID: 6; Handle: 00680000; Type: Segment]
6c0000	6c1000	1000	MEM_PRIVATE	MEM_COMMIT	PAGE_EXECUTE_READWRITE	Heap [ID: 10; Handle: 006c0000; Type: Segment]
6c1000	700000	3f000	MEM_PRIVATE	MEM_RESERVE		Heap [ID: 10; Handle: 006c0000; Type: Segment]
720000	721000	1000	MEM_PRIVATE	MEM_COMMIT	PAGE_EXECUTE_READWRITE	Heap [ID: 4; Handle: 00720000; Type: Segment]
721000	760000	3f000	MEM_PRIVATE	MEM_RESERVE		Heap [ID: 4; Handle: 00720000; Type: Segment]
14b0000	14b1000	1000	MEM_PRIVATE	MEM_COMMIT	PAGE_EXECUTE_READWRITE	Heap [ID: 9; Handle: 014b0000; Type: Segment]
14b1000	14f0000	3f000	MEM_PRIVATE	MEM_RESERVE		Heap [ID: 9; Handle: 014b0000; Type: Segment]

```
0:000> !address /f:IMAGE
```

```
BaseAddr EndAddr+1 RgnSize     Type     State         Protect                          Usage
------------------------------------------------------------------------------------------------
  260000    261000    1000 MEM_IMAGE   MEM_COMMIT  PAGE_READONLY     Image [CH_04; "CH-04.exe"]
  261000    262000    1000 MEM_IMAGE   MEM_RESERVE                   Image [CH_04; "CH-04.exe"]
  262000    263000    1000 MEM_IMAGE   MEM_COMMIT  PAGE_EXECUTE_READ Image [CH_04; "CH-04.exe"]
  263000    264000    1000 MEM_IMAGE   MEM_RESERVE                   Image [CH_04; "CH-04.exe"]
  264000    265000    1000 MEM_IMAGE   MEM_COMMIT  PAGE_READONLY     Image [CH_04; "CH-04.exe"]
  265000    266000    1000 MEM_IMAGE   MEM_RESERVE                   Image [CH_04; "CH-04.exe"]
  266000    267000    1000 MEM_IMAGE   MEM_COMMIT  PAGE_READONLY     Image [CH_04; "CH-04.exe"]
  267000    268000    1000 MEM_IMAGE   MEM_RESERVE                   Image [CH_04; "CH-04.exe"]
55c30000  55c31000    1000 MEM_IMAGE   MEM_COMMIT  PAGE_READONLY     Image [mscorlib_ni;

/*code removed*/

77d87000 77db0000   29000 MEM_IMAGE   MEM_COMMIT  PAGE_READONLY     Image [ADVAPI32; "C:\Windows\
system32\ADVAPI32.dll"]

0:000> !address /f:FILEMap

BaseAddr EndAddr+1 RgnSize     Type     State         Protect                          Usage
------------------------------------------------------------------------------------------------
  180000    1e7000   67000 MEM_MAPPED  MEM_COMMIT  PAGE_READONLY     MappedFile "\Device\
    HarddiskVolume7\Windows\System32\locale.nls"
  1f0000    1f1000    1000 MEM_MAPPED  MEM_COMMIT  PAGE_READWRITE    MappedFile "PageFile"
  200000    210000   10000 MEM_MAPPED  MEM_COMMIT  PAGE_READWRITE    MappedFile "PageFile"
  270000    275000    5000 MEM_MAPPED  MEM_COMMIT  PAGE_READONLY     MappedFile "PageFile"
  275000    330000   bb000 MEM_MAPPED  MEM_RESERVE                   MappedFile "PageFile"
  330000    333000    3000 MEM_MAPPED  MEM_COMMIT  PAGE_READONLY     MappedFile "PageFile"
  333000    338000    5000 MEM_MAPPED  MEM_RESERVE                   MappedFile "PageFile"
  760000    7f8000   98000 MEM_MAPPED  MEM_COMMIT  PAGE_READONLY     MappedFile "PageFile"
  7f8000   1360000  b68000 MEM_MAPPED  MEM_RESERVE                   MappedFile "PageFile"
  37b0000   3a7f000  2cf000 MEM_MAPPED  MEM_COMMIT  PAGE_READONLY     MappedFile "\Device\
    HarddiskVolume7\Windows\Globalization\Sorting\SortDefault.nls"
  3c00000   3ed2000  2d2000 MEM_MAPPED  MEM_COMMIT  PAGE_READONLY     MappedFile "\Device\
    HarddiskVolume7\Windows\Microsoft.NET\Framework\v4.0.30319\sortdefault.nlp"
7f6f5000  7f7f0000   fb000 MEM_MAPPED  MEM_RESERVE                   MappedFile "PageFile"

0:000> !address /f:PEB

BaseAddr EndAddr+1 RgnSize     Type      State        Protect        Usage
------------------------------------------------------------------------------------------------
7ffdd000  7ffde000    1000 MEM_PRIVATE  MEM_COMMIT PAGE_READWRITE PEB  [88c]

0:000> !address /f:TEB

BaseAddr EndAddr+1 RgnSize     Type   State          Protect                          Usage
------------------------------------------------------------------------------------------------
7ffdb000  7ffdc000    1000 MEM_PRIVATE MEM_COMMIT  PAGE_READWRITE    TEB  [~3; 88c.f80]
7ffdc000  7ffdd000    1000 MEM_PRIVATE MEM_COMMIT  PAGE_READWRITE    TEB  [~2; 88c.640]
7ffde000 7ffdf000    1000 MEM_PRIVATE MEM_COMMIT  PAGE_READWRITE    TEB  [~1; 88c.ec4]
7ffdf000 7ffe0000    1000 MEM_PRIVATE MEM_COMMIT  PAGE_READWRITE    TEB  [~0; 88c.fc8]
```

Class Loader in the CLR

When the CLR starts executing an assembly, it executes the contents of the assembly method by method, depending on usage (e.g., if a method from an assembly is never called, it will never be JIT compiled). The CLR uses the threads as the execution unit for executing methods via the OS. When the CLR creates the thread with the associated method, that thread is scheduled by the OS's scheduler to be executed by the OS based on the OS scheduling mechanism, priority, and so on.

Any class from an assembly contains one (considering the default constructor) or more methods. All these methods are either IL or native code (when compiled using ngen.exe) based. The assembly also contains the metadata that define the types in the assembly, which are used by the class loader to load the appropriate IL code into memory to define the type at runtime.

The class loader checks for certain consistency requirements that are vital to the .NET Framework security enforcement mechanism. These checks constitute a minimal, mandatory verification process that precedes the IL verification, which is more rigorous (although optional). In addition, the class loader supports security enforcement by providing some of the credentials required for validating code identity. The CLR allows only one class loader—its own. The .NET Framework does not support user-written class loaders.

Type-safe programs only reference memory that has been allocated for their use, and they access objects only through their public interfaces. These two restrictions allow objects to safely share a single address space, and they guarantee that security checks conducted by the objects' interfaces are not circumvented. Code access security, the CLR's security mechanism, can effectively protect code from unauthorized access only if there is a way to verify that the code is type safe. To meet this need, the CLR uses the information in type signatures to help determine whether MSIL code is type safe. The CLR checks to see that the metadata are well formed, and it performs control flow analyses to make sure that certain structural and behavioral conditions are met. The runtime declares that a program is successfully verified only if it is type safe. Used in conjunction with the strong typing of metadata and MSIL, such checking can ensure the type safety of programs written in MSIL. The .NET Framework requires code to be so checked before it is run, unless a specific (administratively controlled) security check determines that the code can be fully trusted.

Locating the Main Entry Point

When the CLR loads an assembly to execute for the first time, it requires that the main entry point (usually the Main method) of that assembly be located. The class loader will locate the class that contains the entry point and load that into the memory. If you look at the stack trace of the CLR while debugging, using WinDbg, you will find that the Class loader from the CLR will execute the RunMain method to execute the Main method from current running assembly. The following stack trace was captured while debugging the previous listing, using WinDbg, to show how the CLR calls RunMain method:

```
0:000> !eestack -short
---------------------------------------------
Thread   0
Current frame: ntdll!KiFastSystemCallRet
ChildEBP RetAddr  Caller, Callee
002fe3a4 774d507c ntdll!ZwMapViewOfSection+0xc

/*removed*/

002ff080 587cce82 clr!ClassLoader::RunMain+0x24c, calling clr!MethodDescCallSite::CallWithValueTypes
002ff180 586ee30a clr!MethodDesc::GetSigFromMetadata+0x21
002ff1e4 587ccf90 clr!Assembly::ExecuteMainMethod+0xc1, calling clr!ClassLoader::RunMain

/*removed*/

---------------------------------------------
Thread   2
```

The class loader performs its function the first time a type has been referenced. The class loader loads .NET classes into memory and prepares them for execution. Before it can successfully do this, however, it must locate the target class. To ascertain the target class, the class loader looks in different places, including the application configuration file (.config) in the current directory, the global assembly cache (GAC), and the metadata that are part of the PE file, specifically the manifest. The information that is provided by one or more of these items is crucial for locating the correct target class. Recall that a class can be scoped to a particular namespace, a namespace can be scoped to a particular assembly, and an assembly can be scoped to a specific version. Given this, two classes, both named Car, are treated as different types, even if the version information of their assemblies is the same. Once the class loader has found and loaded the target class, it caches the type information for the class so that it does not have to load the class again for the duration of this process. By caching this information, the class loader will later determine how much memory has to be allocated for the newly created instance of this class.

Stub Code for the Classes

Once the target class is loaded, the class loader injects a small stub, such as a function prologue, into every method of the loaded class.

This stub is used for two purposes: to denote the status of the JIT compilation and to transition between managed and unmanaged code.

At this point, if the loaded class references other types, and those referenced types have already been loaded, the class loader will do nothing; otherwise, the it will try to load the referenced types. As Figure 6-5 demonstrates, the class loader loads the type-related information, such as IL code and metadata, into memory; maps it to virtual memory; and sets it to a state that can be used by the CLR to start JIT compilation when needed during execution.

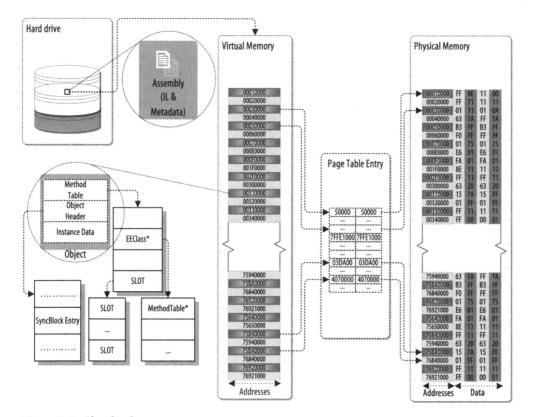

Figure 6-5. *Class loader*

Finally, the class loader uses the appropriate metadata to initialize the static variables and instantiate an object of the loaded class.

Verification

Type verification is done at runtime; after the class loader has loaded a class and before a piece of IL code can execute, the verifier starts searching for code that must be verified. By verifying type safety at runtime, the CLR can prevent the execution of code that is not type safe and ensure that the code is used as intended and not illegally. In short, type safety means more reliability. Let's discuss where the verifier fits within the CLR.

The verifier is responsible for verifying that

- The metadata are well formed (i.e., valid)

- The IL code is type safe (i.e., the type signatures are used correctly)

Both of these criteria must be met before the code can be executed, because JIT compilation will take place only when code and metadata have been successfully verified.

In addition to checking for type safety, the verifier also performs control-flow analysis of the code to ensure that it is using types correctly. You should note that because the verifier is a part of the JIT compiler, it kicks in only when a method is being invoked, not when a class or assembly is loaded. You should note as well that verification is an optional step, as trusted code will never be verified, but will be immediately directed to the JIT compiler for compilation (more details about the verification algorithm can be found in the ECMA C# specification IL, which is available on the ECMA web site [http://www.ecma-international.org/publications/standards/Ecma-335.htm]).

Conclusion

The CLR executes any application written using a .NET language. The compiled code of an application resides in the assembly as IL code, unless the assembly is precompiled. To be executed by the CLR virtual execution environment, the IL code residing in the assembly must be JIT compiled into the native code. To accomplish this, the CLR uses the JIT compiler, compiling the IL code into the native code at runtime. In the next chapter, you will learn about JIT compilation, including how it takes place in the virtual execution environment during execution of the assembly. You will be using the tool WinDbg to explore this.

Further Reading

Box, Don. Essential .NET: The Common Language Runtime. Vol. 1. Boston: Addison-Wesley, 2003.

Hewardt, Mario. Advanced .NET Debugging. Upper Saddle River, NJ: Addison-Wesley, 2010.

Miller, James S., and Susann Ragsdale. The Common Language Infrastructure Annotated Standard. Boston: Addison-Wesley, 2004.

Richter, Jeffrey. CLR via C#, Second Edition. Redmond, WA: Microsoft, 2006.

CHAPTER 7

CLR Execution Model II

The CLR execution model contains different components for implementation. As you saw in Chapter 6, the assembly loader of the CLR is used to load the assembly, which contains the IL code and metadata for the application that is executing the CLR. The class loader component loads any type defined in the application assembly or external types that reside in other assemblies. When the types are laid out in the memory, the execution engine can execute the code of that assembly. But, as mentioned earlier, the IL code is not directly executable by the CPU but rather requires compiling into native code. The CLR component piece that does this is called the JIT compiler. In this chapter, you will learn about the JIT compiler.

JIT Compilation

The execution engine is the critical component of the CLR that uses the JIT compiler to compile the CIL code into native code. How and when the CIL code is compiled into native code are not specified as part of the standard, and those determinations rest with the implementation of the CLR, but all goes on demand.

There are many advantages to JIT compilation, among the most important being code optimization and portability. The JIT compiler can dynamically compile code that is optimized for the target machine. For example, if you take a .NET assembly from a single processor–based machine to a multiprocessor–based machine, the JIT compiler on the latter knows about the multi-processor and may be able to spit out native code that takes advantage of it.

Method Stub of a Type

Each CTS type contains a method table to hold all the methods defined by that type. The method table of a type includes all the methods that have been inherited from its base class as well as its own defined methods. To explore this, let's look at the following, simple example, in which the WinDbg tool is used to display the method table of the Program class:

```
using System;

namespace CH_07
{
    class Program
    {
        static void Main(string[] args)
        {
            Book book = new Book();
            book.Print();
            Console.ReadLine();
        }
    }
}
```

```
    public class Book
    {
        public void Print()
        {
            Console.WriteLine(ToString());
        }
    }
}
```

The Program class has only the Main method on its own, but this class inherited three other methods from its base class, object. When this application is compiled into an assembly (CH_07.exe), using csc.exe, then you load this assembly into WinDbg to start debugging. You will be using the following WinDbg command to initialize the debugging session:

```
0:000> sxe ld clrjit
0:000> g
0:000> .loadby sos clr
0:000> .load C:\Windows\Microsoft.NET\Framework\v4.0.30319\sos.dll
```

After initializing the session, execute the !dumpMT command, along with the -MD option, to display a list of all the methods defined by the object type. To do this, you need to get the relevant method table address of the Program class, which can be extracted, using the !name2ee command, by providing the assembly name and class name as parameters, as show:

```
0:000> !name2ee CH_07.exe CH_07.Program
Module:        00462e9c
Assembly:      CH_07.exe
Token:         02000002
MethodTable:   00463814
EEClass:       00461418
Name:          CH_07.Program
```

Now, you can use the MethodTable address, along with the !dumpmt command, to examine the method table of the Program class. From the output of the !dumpMT command, you can see that the Program class has defined the Main method and the default constructor, .ctor. Neither method has been JIT compiled yet, but the methods the Program class inherited from the object class have been (see the output marked "PreJIT"):

```
0:000> !dumpmt -MD 00463814

/*removed*/

MethodDesc Table
    Entry MethodDesc      JIT Name

/*Following method inherited by the Object class*/
55faa7e0    55d84934    PreJIT System.Object.ToString()
55fae2e0    55d8493c    PreJIT System.Object.Equals(System.Object)
55fae1f0    55d8495c    PreJIT System.Object.GetHashCode()
56031600    55d84970    PreJIT System.Object.Finalize()
```

```
/*Following method defined by the Program class*/
0046c015    0046380c    NONE CH_07.Program..ctor()
0046c011    00463800    NONE CH_07.Program.Main(System.String[])
```

The CLR allocates a block of memory for each of the methods of a type. This block of memory contains information about the method, including its code. The code block holds a pointer to a memory address that points to another memory region. This memory region contains the implementation code for that method and is known as a slot for that type. The collection of slots for a single type is called its virtual table (vtable). All vtable slots have an instruction to a method prestub to tell the CLR to JIT compile as needed.

In a .NET application, three kinds of JIT compilation status are used to control the JIT compilation:

- PreJIT: In the PreJIT state the IL code has been compiled into native code before the assembly is executed by the CLR.

- JIT: The JIT compiler compiles the IL code and stores it on the code heap. After the JIT compilation the JIT compiler updates the memory location with the address of the method for which the JIT compiler has been triggered.

- NONE: In this state the IL code has not been compiled into native code, but each of the methods that has a status of NONE has a method prestub that calls the JIT compiler.

To understand how these three options control and maintain the JIT compilation process in .NET, first you need to learn how the JIT compiler compiles. In the following sections you will use the same debugging session you employed previously to advance your understanding of the JIT compilation process.

JIT-Compiled Status: NONE

At runtime if the status of the method of a type is set to NONE, that method must be JIT compiled. It is important that the CLR is aware of such methods. In the class-loading step the class loader adds a piece of code known as the stub code to each of the methods that has not yet been JIT compiled, or that has a JIT status of NONE. To find these methods, you will set a break point at the Main method and let the execution continue for the previous debugging session, using the g command:

```
!bpmd CH_07.exe CH_07.Program.Main
g
```

Note that this method already has IL code, so do not confuse the two. The IL code is produced at the front-end compile time by the C# compiler, which embeds the IL code into the assembly. You can use the !dumpmt command to learn the method description address for each of the methods for the Book class:

```
0:000> !name2ee CH_07.exe CH_07.Book
Module:         00462e9c
Assembly:       CH_07.exe
Token:          02000003
MethodTable:    00463880
EEClass:        00461484
Name:           CH_07.Book

0:000> !dumpmt -MD 00463880
EEClass:        00461484
Module:         00462e9c
Name:           CH_07.Book
mdToken:        02000003
```

```
File:           J:\Book\C# Deconstructed\SourceCode\Chapters\CH_07\bin\Debug\CH_07.exe
BaseSize:       0xc
ComponentSize:  0x0
Slots in VTable: 6
Number of IFaces in IFaceMap: 0
---------------------------------------
MethodDesc Table
   Entry MethodDesc      JIT Name
55faa7e0  55d84934    PreJIT System.Object.ToString()
55fae2e0  55d8493c    PreJIT System.Object.Equals(System.Object)
55fae1f0  55d8495c    PreJIT System.Object.GetHashCode()
56031600  55d84970    PreJIT System.Object.Finalize()

0046c041  00463878     NONE CH_07.Book..ctor()
0046c03d  0046386c     NONE CH_07.Book.Print()
```

Now, the !dumpil command will show the relevant IL code for the relevant method:

```
!dumpil 55d84934
!dumpil 55d8493c
!dumpil 51dc495c
!dumpil 55d84970
!dumpil 00463878
!dumpil 0046386c
```

The IL output is as follows:

```
0:000> !dumpil 55d84934
ilAddr = 5749ba8a
IL_0000: ldarg.0
/*removed*/

0:000> !dumpil 55d8493c
ilAddr = 5749ba97
IL_0000: ldarg.0
/*removed*/

0:000> !dumpil 51dc495c
ilAddr = 5749baa6
IL_0000: ldarg.0
/*removed*/

0:000> !dumpil 55d84970
ilAddr = 5749ba88
IL_0000: ret

0:000> !dumpil 00463878
ilAddr = 00182070
/*removed*/
IL_0006: ret
```

```
0:000> !dumpil 0046386c
ilAddr = 00182050
IL_0000: nop
/*removed*/
```

In addition, each of the methods with a JIT status of NONE will point to a memory block that contains a method call to the PrestubMethodFrame method. If you study this method, you will find that it contains jmp instructions (in each slot for the type) to jump into a shared piece of code, called the PreJIT stub. This stub is responsible for invoking the JIT compiler (which resides in mscorjit.dll) to generate native code for the method from which it has been called. To see how the PreJIT stub calls the PrestubMethodFrame, you can disassemble all the methods from the method table, using the !u command:

```
!u 0034c041
!u 0034c03d

0:000> !u 0034c041
Unmanaged code
/*removed*/
001ac024 e927480400        jmp     00ae0850
/*removed*/

0:000> !u 0046c03d
Unmanaged code
/*removed*/
001ac024 e927480400        jmp     0046c045
/*removed*/

!u 00ae0850
!u 0046c045

0:000> !u 00ae0850
Unmanaged code
001f0850 50                push    eax
001f0851 52                push    edx
001f0852 682037fe57        push    offset clr!PrestubMethodFrame::`vftable' (57fe3720)
/*removed*/

0:000> !u 0046c045
Unmanaged code
001f0850 50                push    eax
001f0851 52                push    edx
001f0852 682037fe57        push    offset clr!PrestubMethodFrame::`vftable' (57fe3720)
/*removed*/
```

Figure 7-1 demonstrates the JIT compilation for those methods with a JIT status of NONE.

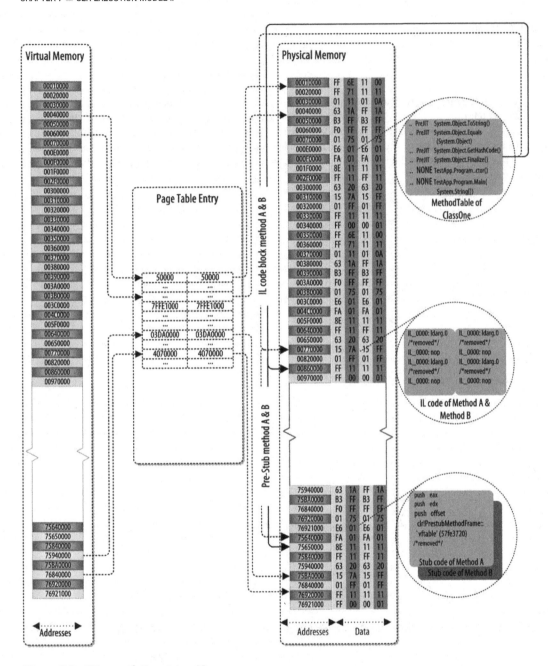

Figure 7-1. *JIT compilation status: None*

At a later time, those methods that have a JIT status of NONE will be JIT compiled into native code by the JIT compiler. When the JIT compiler compiles these methods, it produces the native code, stores the compiled native code in the code Heap region of the memory, and then updates the stub code for the methods to point to this memory location.

JIT-Compiled Status: JIT

All slots that have already been JIT compiled contain an unconditional jmp to the target JIT-compiled code in their instruction section. Having a jmp in the slot enables fast execution of calls, with the overhead of only a single jmp instruction. To explore this, run the following command, using the WinDbg tool:

```
0:000> !bpmd CH_07.exe CH_07.Book.Print
0:000> g
```

```
0:000>  !dumpmt -MD 00463880
EEClass:        00461484
Module:         00462e9c
Name:           CH_07.Book
mdToken:        02000003
File:           J:\Book\C# Deconstructed\SourceCode\Chapters\CH_07\bin\Debug\CH_07.exe
BaseSize:       0xc
ComponentSize:  0x0
Slots in VTable: 6
Number of IFaces in IFaceMap: 0
--------------------------------------
MethodDesc Table
   Entry MethodDesc      JIT Name
55faa7e0   55d84934   PreJIT System.Object.ToString()
55fae2e0   55d8493c   PreJIT System.Object.Equals(System.Object)
55fae1f0   55d8495c   PreJIT System.Object.GetHashCode()
56031600   55d84970   PreJIT System.Object.Finalize()

006700d0   00463878      JIT CH_07.Book..ctor()
00670110   0046386c      JIT CH_07.Book.Print()
```

As you can see, those methods that had a JIT status of NONE are compiled, and their status is updated to JIT.

Next, by disassembling these methods, you will find that each of these methods jumps to a memory location where the JIT compiler has stored the compiled native code:

```
u 006700d0
u 00670110
```

```
0:000> u 006700d0
006700d0 55                  push    ebp
006700d1 8bec                mov     ebp,esp
006700d3 50                  push    eax
006700d4 894dfc              mov     dword ptr [ebp-4],ecx
006700d7 833d3c31460000      cmp     dword ptr ds:[46313Ch],0
006700de 7405                je      006700e5
006700e0 e86a5a7956          call    clr!JIT_DbgIsJustMyCode (56e05b4f)
006700e5 8b4dfc              mov     ecx,dword ptr [ebp-4]
```

```
0:000> u 00670110
00670110 55              push    ebp
00670111 8bec            mov     ebp,esp
00670113 83ec08          sub     esp,8
00670116 894dfc          mov     dword ptr [ebp-4],ecx
00670119 833d3c31460000  cmp     dword ptr ds:[46313Ch],0
00670120 7405            je      00670127
00670122 e8285a7956      call    clr!JIT_DbgIsJustMyCode (56e05b4f)
00670127 90              nop
```

From the this disassembled code, if you look at the instruction details of the memory addresses 006700e5 and 00670127, you will see that they are pointing to the JIT-compiled native code:

```
0:000> u 006700e5
004700ea 8b4dfc          mov     ecx,dword ptr [ebp-4]
004700ed e88e6df956      call    mscorlib_ni+0x2b6e80 (57406e80)
/*removed*/
```

```
0:000> u 00670127
00470135 90              nop
00470136 8b45fc          mov     eax,dword ptr [ebp-4]
00470139 8b4804          mov     ecx,dword ptr [eax+4]
0047013c e86b6ff356      call    mscorlib_ni+0x2570ac (573a70ac)
/*removed*/
```

Here is more explicit code:

```
0:000> !u 006700e5
Normal JIT generated code
CH_07.Book..ctor()
Begin 006700d0, size 22
006700d0 55
/*removed*/
004700ed e88e6df956 call mscorlib_ni+0x2b6e80 (57406e80) (System.Object..ctor(), mdToken: 06000001)
/*removed*/
```

```
0:000> !u 00670127
Normal JIT generated code
CH_07.Book.Print()
Begin 00670110, size 33

/*removed*/
0047013c e86b6ff356 call mscorlib_ni+0x2570ac (573a70ac) (System.Console.WriteLine(System.String),
mdToken: 06000919)
/*removed*/
```

Figure 7-2 demonstrates the JIT compilation for those methods that have a JIT status of JIT. The JIT-compiled methods point to the memory location, which is simply the address of the memory section that contains the native code for the method.

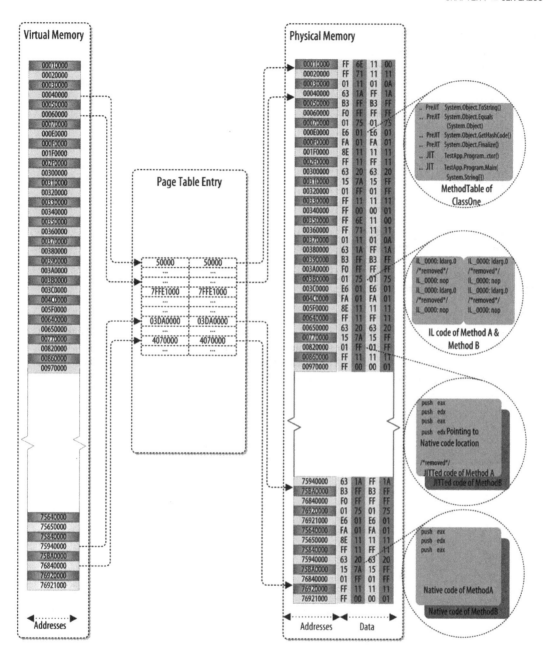

Figure 7-2. *JIT compilation status: JIT*

JIT-Compiled Status: PreJIT

As mentioned earlier, PreJIT status is accorded to those methods that have already been compiled by other tools, such as ngen.exe, and that do not require JIT compilation at runtime. The following output reveals the PreJIT status of the inherited methodsis:

```
0:000> !name2ee CH_07.exe CH_07.Program
/*removed*/
MethodTable: 00463814
/*removed*/


0:000> !dumpmt -MD 00463814
/*removed*/
MethodDesc Table
   Entry MethodDesc      JIT Name
55faa7e0   55d84934    PreJIT System.Object.ToString()
55fae2e0   55d8493c    PreJIT System.Object.Equals(System.Object)
55fae1f0   55d8495c    PreJIT System.Object.GetHashCode()
56031600   55d84970    PreJIT System.Object.Finalize()
/*removed*/
```

These PreJIT methods have been compiled earlier. The assembly was then loaded into the memory by the tool ngen.exe. This tool generates native code and embeds it into the assembly. At runtime the class loader loads the native code and stores it on the memory heap, from where it can be accessed. Figure 7-3 illustrates the methods that have a status of PreJIT. The native code for these methods does not call the JIT compiler, but it contains direct native code.

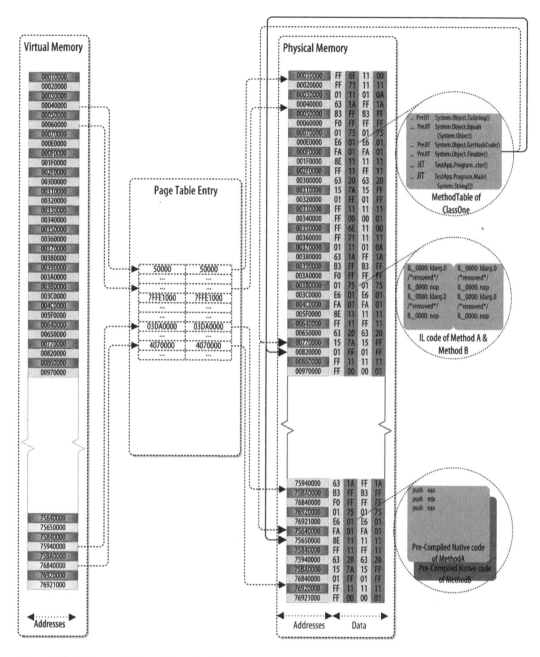

Figure 7-3. *JIT compilation status: PreJIT*

You can explore further by examining this code:

```
u 55d84934
u 55d8493c
u 55d8495c
u 55d84970
```

```
0:000> u 55d84934
mscorlib_ni+0x4934:
55d84934 0200            add     al,byte ptr [eax]
55d84936 1d11003800      sbb     eax,380011h
55d8493b 0003            add     byte ptr [ebx],al
55d8493d 001f            add     byte ptr [edi],bl
55d8493f 1101            adc     dword ptr [ecx],eax
55d84941 b400            mov     ah,0
55d84943 000400          add     byte ptr [eax+eax],al
55d84946 21510a          and     dword ptr [ecx+0Ah],edx

0:000> u 55d8493c
mscorlib_ni+0x493c:
55d8493c 0300            add     eax,dword ptr [eax]
55d8493e 1f         .    pop     ds
55d8493f 1101            adc     dword ptr [ecx],eax
55d84941 b400            mov     ah,0
55d84943 000400          add     byte ptr [eax+eax],al
55d84946 21510a          and     dword ptr [ecx+0Ah],edx
55d84949 b420            mov     ah,20h
55d8494b 2014b7          and     byte ptr [edi+esi*4],dl

0:000> u 55d8495c
mscorlib_ni+0x495c:
55d8495c 06              push    es
55d8495d 0027            add     byte ptr [edi],ah
55d8495f 1102            adc     dword ptr [edx],eax
55d84961 b000            mov     al,0
55d84963 0007            add     byte ptr [edi],al
55d84965 0029            add     byte ptr [ecx],ch
55d84967 3305dc012001    xor     eax,dword ptr ds:[12001DCh]
55d8496d 005000          add     byte ptr [eax],dl

0:000> u 55d84970
mscorlib_ni+0x4970:
55d84970 0800            or      byte ptr [eax],al
55d84972 2c11            sub     al,11h
55d84974 035c0000        add     ebx,dword ptr [eax+eax]
55d84978 0900            or      dword ptr [eax],eax
55d8497a 2e3306          xor     eax,dword ptr cs:[esi]
55d8497d d801            fadd    dword ptr [ecx]
55d8497f 200400          and     byte ptr [eax+eax],al
55d84982 50              push    eax
```

None of the native code shown calls the JIT compiler, as the code has already been compiled.

Unfortunately, the CLR JIT compiler has to lose some intelligence in favor of code generation speed. Remember, the JIT compiler is actually compiling your code as the application runs, so producing code that executes fast is not always as important as producing code fast that executes.

How Many Times a Method Is JIT Compiled

During the subsequent invocations of the same method, no JIT compilation is needed, because each time the CLR reads the information in the stub, it sees the address of the native method. The JIT compiler performs its trick the first time a method is invoked. If the method is never required at runtime, it will never be JIT compiled. The compiled native code stays in memory until the process shuts down and the GC clears off all references and memory associated with the process.

In Chapter 6, you looked at how the CLR uses the assembly loader to load an assembly into memory, the class loader component of the CLR to load requested class into memory, and the JIT compiler to compile managed code into native code as required.

As discussed previously, the CLR executes an assembly method by method. Whenever the CLR executes a method, it will use a mechanism to maintain the current state of the method and move to execute the calling method. With the calling method the CLR will also maintain method state, and in this method state will be information to return to the point from which it has been called. When it finishes execution of the calling method, the CLR will return to the called method and resume its execution. In the following section, you will study the method state and how the CLR handles it while executing a method.

Execution State of the CLR

The CLR is responsible for choosing the best way to call a method, lay out the stack, and maintain the method state. The CLR achieves this abstraction by implementing a mechanism to maintain the global state and method state while executing a .NET application.

The CLR maintains the method state by introducing a linked list of method states known as a thread of control. When the CLR creates a new method state, it is linked to the current method state.

The method state describes the environment in which a method executes (in conventional compiler terminology the method state corresponds to a superset of the information captured in the invocation stack frame). The .NET Framework method state consists of the following items:

- Instruction pointer (IP): This is used to store the next IL instruction to be executed.

- Evaluation stack: The CLR uses nonaddressable memory block upon method execution. This block of memory is preserved during other method calls from the currently executing method.

- Local variable array (starting at index 0): During method execution all the local variables employed in the method use this area to preserve their values.

- Argument array (starting at index 0): This is used to store the values of the current method's incoming arguments.

- methodInfo handle: This contains read-only information about the method. In particular, the methodInfo handle holds the signature of the method, the types of its local variables, and data about its exception handlers.

- Local memory pool: The CLR uses addressable memory from the local memory pool for dynamic object allocation and reclaimes memory pool upon method context termination.

- Return state handle: During method switching the CLR uses this mechanism to store the current context information of the executing method; set up the new method state of the calling method; and, upon return, restore the previously stored method state.

- Security descriptor: This is used by the .NET Framework security system to record security override.

Figure 7-4 illustrates the machine state model, which includes threads of control, method states, and multiple heaps in a shared address space. The method state is an abstraction of the stack frame. Arguments and local variables are part of the method state, but they can contain object references that refer to data stored in any of the managed heaps. The method state is laid out, using the concept of the Stack by allocated address space. The CLR allocates this address space from the address space used for the current process.

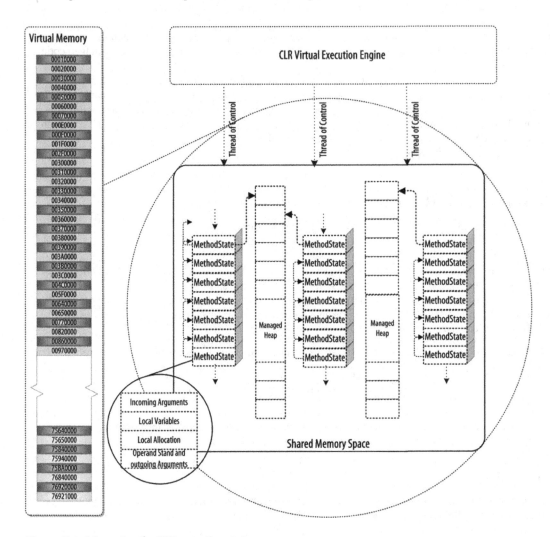

Figure 7-4. *Managing the CLR execution state*

Let's look at CLR method state usage, using the following source code:

```
using System;

namespace CH_07
{
    class Program
    {
        static void Main(string[] args){}
    }
}
```

Once this application is compiled into an assembly (CH_07.exe), using csc.exe, you load the assembly into WinDbg to start debugging. You will be using the following WinDbg command to initialize the debugging session:

```
0:000> sxe ld clrjit
0:000> g
0:000> .loadby sos clr
0:000> .load C:\Windows\Microsoft.NET\Framework\v4.0.30319\sos.dll
```

Once the application is compiled into App.exe, using csc.exe, and loaded via WinDbg, you are ready to perform a new experiment to explore how threads and method state are generated. By inputting the ~* command, you will see the list of threads this assembly is using at runtime:

```
0:000> ~*
.  0  Id: 15b8.1564 Suspend: 1 Teb: 7ffdf000 Unfrozen
      Start: mscoree!_CorExeMain_Exported (79004ddb)
      Priority: 0  Priority class: 32  Affinity: 1
   1  Id: 15b8.110 Suspend: 1 Teb: 7ffde000 Unfrozen
      Start: clr!DebuggerRCThread::ThreadProcStatic (7929d0f4)
      Priority: 0  Priority class: 32  Affinity: 1
   2  Id: 15b8.16b8 Suspend: 1 Teb: 7ffdd000 Unfrozen
      Start: clr!Thread::intermediateThreadProc (792464f8)
      Priority: 2  Priority class: 32  Affinity: 1
```

Note   The first line of this output, 0, is the decimal thread number, 4DC is the hexadecimal process ID, 470 is the hexadecimal thread ID, 0x7FFDE000 is the address of the TEB, and Unfrozen is the thread status. The period (.) before thread 1 means that this thread is the current thread. The number sign (#) before thread 2 means that this thread was the one that originally caused the exception or that it was active when the debugger attached to the process.

This output shows that a few threads were created to execute this application. Each of these threads has an associated frame. So, thread 15b8 will create a MethodState frame and execute the different methods Let's look at an example that explains the behavior of the method state used by the CLR to handle the execution of an application:

```csharp
using System;

namespace Ch_07
{
    class Program
    {
        static void Main(string[] args)
        {
            ClassTest ct = new ClassTest();
            ct.One();
        }
    }

    public class ClassTest
    {
        public void One() {
            Console.WriteLine("Hello World");
        }
        public void Two() { }
        public void Three() { }
    }
}
```

Once this application is compiled into an assembly (CH_07.exe), you load the assembly into WinDbg to start debugging. You will be using the following WinDbg command to initialize the debugging session:

```
0:000> sxe ld clrjit
0:000> g
0:000> .loadby sos clr
0:000> .load C:\Windows\Microsoft.NET\Framework\v4.0.30319\sos.dll
```

When a C# application is executed by the CLR, the CLR uses the concept of the stack frame. With each method call the CLR creates a frame and stores on the stack frame:

```
!bpmd Ch_07.exe   Ch_07.Program.Main
!bpmd Ch_07.exe   Ch_07.ClassTest.One
g
```

During execution of the previous program, when the CLR executes method One, by calling it from the Main method, the CLR creates an activation frame for each of the method calls. The CLR maintains the method state for each method call. For example, when the CLR calls the Main method from the clr!CallDescrWorker+0x33 method, it creates an activation frame for storing the method state for the clr!CallDescrWorker+0x33 method so that it can be resume the clr!CallDescrWorker+0x33 execution when the Main method finishes its execution by restoring the previous state.

The CLR uses the same technique for a process from start to finish. The following !for_each_frame command output demonstrates how the CLR maintains the state of the method call from the beginning of the execution:

```
0:000> !for_each_frame r

_ _ _ _ _ _ _ _ _ _ _ _ _ _ _
00 0014f170 005000b4 0x500110
eax=0044386c ebx=00000000 ecx=0198b684 edx=003278e8 esi=003278e8 edi=0014f1b0
eip=00500110 esp=0014f174 ebp=0014f184 iopl=0         nv up ei pl nz ac po nc
cs=001b  ss=0023  ds=0023  es=0023  fs=003b  gs=0000              efl=00000212
00500110 55              push    ebp

_ _ _ _ _ _ _ _ _ _ _ _ _ _ _
01 0014f184 60db21db 0x5000b4
eax=0044386c ebx=00000000 ecx=0198b684 edx=003278e8 esi=003278e8 edi=0014f1b0
eip=00500110 esp=0014f174 ebp=0014f184 iopl=0         nv up ei pl nz ac po nc
cs=001b  ss=0023  ds=0023  es=0023  fs=003b  gs=0000              efl=00000212
00500110 55              push    ebp

_ _ _ _ _ _ _ _ _ _ _ _ _ _ _
02 0014f194 60dd4a2a clr!CallDescrWorker+0x33
eax=0044386c ebx=00000000 ecx=0198b684 edx=003278e8 esi=003278e8 edi=0014f1b0
eip=00500110 esp=0014f174 ebp=0014f184 iopl=0         nv up ei pl nz ac po nc
cs=001b  ss=0023  ds=0023  es=0023  fs=003b  gs=0000              efl=00000212
00500110 55              push    ebp

_ _ _ _ _ _ _ _ _ _ _ _ _ _ _
03 0014f210 60dd4bcc clr!CallDescrWorkerWithHandler+0x8e
eax=0044386c ebx=00000000 ecx=0198b684 edx=003278e8 esi=003278e8 edi=0014f1b0
eip=00500110 esp=0014f174 ebp=0014f184 iopl=0         nv up ei pl nz ac po nc
cs=001b  ss=0023  ds=0023  es=0023  fs=003b  gs=0000              efl=00000212
00500110 55              push    ebp

_ _ _ _ _ _ _ _ _ _ _ _ _ _ _
/* code removed*/

_ _ _ _ _ _ _ _ _ _ _ _ _ _ _
00 0014f170 005000b4 0x500110
```

From the prior output you can see that upon calling the clr!CallDescrWorkerWithHandler+0x8e method, the CLR stores the method state at the activation frame number 03, as well as the return address (60dd4bcc), so that when it finishes with the clr!CallDescrWorkerWithHandler+0x8e method, it can return to the place from which it has been called (60dd4bcc). Similarly, clr!CallDescrWorker+0x33 returns to 60dd4a2a, the Main method (located in region of the address 0x5000b4) also stores the return address 60db21db on its activation frame, and, finally, the One method of the TestClass class (which is located in the region of 0x500110) stores the return address 005000b4.

!FOR_EACH_FRAME

To get native code and see where it is being called from and where it will return to, you can use the following code:

```
!for_each_frame .echo [${@#ReturnAddress}] [${@#SymbolName}] [${@#SymbolAddress}]
!for_each_frame -?
```

As mentioned earlier, the One method (0x500110) returns to 005000b4, so if you look at the disassembled code of the One method; you will see that when it finishes its execution, it returns to the 005000b4 address:

```
0:000> !u 0x500110
Normal JIT generated code
Ch_07.ClassTest.One()
Begin 00500110, size 27

J:\Book\C# Deconstructed\SourceCode\Chapters\CH_07\Program.cs @ 17:
>>>00500110 55              push    ebp
00500111 8bec               mov     ebp,esp
00500113 50                 push    eax

/* code removed*/

00500136 c3                 ret
```

Likewise, the One (0x500110) method is called just before the 005000b4 address, so if you disassemble the native code located near the 005000b4-10 address, you can determine whether the method residing in the region of the address 0x500110 has been called from this method to reside near 005000b4:

The address 005000b4 resides in the Main method of the Program class, as shown in the following disassembled code:

```
0:000> !u 005000b4-10
Normal JIT generated code
Ch_07.Program.Main(System.String[])
Begin 00500070, size 4a

J:\Book\C# Deconstructed\SourceCode\Chapters\CH_07\Program.cs @ 8:
00500070 55              push    ebp
00500071 8bec               mov     ebp,esp
00500073 83ec0c             sub     esp,0Ch

/* code removed*/

005000ae ff1574384400    call    dword ptr ds:[443874h] (Ch_07.ClassTest.One(), mdToken: 06000003)
005000b4 90              nop

J:\Book\C# Deconstructed\SourceCode\Chapters\CH_07\Program.cs @ 11:
005000b5 90              nop
005000b6 8be5            mov     esp,ebp
005000b8 5d              pop     ebp
005000b9 c3              ret
```

As you can see, at the offset 005000ae, the One method from the ClassTest has been called, and the address 005000b4 follows the method call. From the !for_each_frame output, the address 005000b4 is used as the return address for the frame 00, allocated for the One (0x500110) method.

The same technique has been used for the Main method. Looking at the disassembled code of the method residing in the 60db21db address, you will find that the Main method has been called at the offset 60db21d8 and uses the offset 60db21db as the return address when the CLR finishes with the Main method:

```
0:000> !u 60db21db-10
Unmanaged code
60db21cb ff30            push    dword ptr [eax]

/* code removed*/

60db21d8 ff5518          call    dword ptr [ebp+18h]

60db21db 8b4d14          mov     ecx,dword ptr [ebp+14h]

60db21de 83f904          cmp     ecx,4
60db21e1 7407            je      clr!CallDescrWorker+0x42 (60db21ea)
```

The same is true of the clr!CallDescrWorker+0x33 method call, in which the frame 02 is allocated when the clr!CallDescrWorker+0x33 method is called, as shown in the following disassembled code:

```
0:000> !u 60dd4a2a-10
Unmanaged code
60dd4a1a 7514            jne     clr!CallDescrWorkerWithHandler+0x94 (60dd4a30)
/* code removed*/
60dd4a25 e87ed7fdff      call    clr!CallDescrWorker (60db21a8)

60dd4a2a 8945c8          mov     dword ptr [ebp-38h],eax

60dd4a2d 8955cc          mov     dword ptr [ebp-34h],edx
60dd4a30 897de0          mov     dword ptr [ebp-20h],edi
60dd4a33 8b55e0          mov     edx,dword ptr [ebp-20h]
60dd4a36 8b12            mov     edx,dword ptr [edx]
```

As Figure 7-5 illustrates, the clr!CallDescrWorkerWithHandler+0x8e method calls the clr!CallDescrWorker+0x33 method, which calls the Main method, and the Main method calls the One method from the TestClass. With each of these calls, the CLR maintains the method state to store the current state of the executing method so that when it finishes with the calling method, it can resume with the callee method.

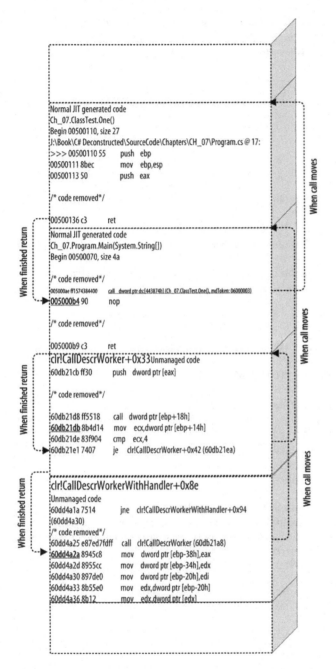

Figure 7-5. *CLR activation frame while executing methods*

Note that I have described the four areas of the method state—incoming arguments array, local variables array, local memory pool, and evaluation stack—as if they were logically distinct areas. This is important, because it is a specification of the CLR architecture. However, in practice, the CLR may actually map these areas in one contiguous array of memory, held as a conventional stack frame on the underlying, target architecture.

Conclusion

We have come to the end of the book. In it, you have explored the basic structure of the computer system, such as what computer architecture is and how the CPU works to execute instructions. In Chapter 1, you learned about the the OS and how it manages the underlying hardware to provide application interfaces that allow the application developer to write applications. In Chapter 2, you were introduced to the concept of programming language. Because of the various platform issues, an application built for one system will not execute on a different platform; this gave rise to the need for the virtual machine. This concept is used in programming language to implement a virtual execution environment, such as the CLR. In Chapter 3, you discovered that the CLR understands IL code and metadata while executing a .NET application. To package these and have them executed by the CLR, there is a standard mechanism called the assembly. In Chapters 4 and 5 you examined memory, as this is the place where your application stays while being executed by the CLR. In Chapters 6 and 7, you considered CLR execution, including the JIT compiler. Overall, the book gave you a high-level overview of the .NET application execution life cycle, from computer architecture to the CLR.

Further Reading

Box, Don. Essential .NET: The Common Language Runtime. Vol. 1. Boston: Addison-Wesley, 2003.

Richter, Jeffrey. CLR via C#. Second Edition. Redmond, WA: Microsoft, 2006.

Hewardt, M. Advanced .NET Debugging. Upper Saddle River, NJ: Pearson, 2010.

Miller, James S., and Susann Ragsdale, S. The Common Language Infrastructure Annotated Standard.
    Boston: Addison-Wesley, 2004.

Index

Get the eBook for only $10!

> Now you can take the weightless companion with you anywhere, anytime. Your purchase of this book entitles you to 3 electronic versions for only $10.

This Apress title will prove so indispensible that you'll want to carry it with you everywhere, which is why we are offering the eBook in 3 formats for only $10 if you have already purchased the print book.

Convenient and fully searchable, the PDF version enables you to easily find and copy code—or perform examples by quickly toggling between instructions and applications. The MOBI format is ideal for your Kindle, while the ePUB can be utilized on a variety of mobile devices.

Go to www.apress.com/promo/tendollars to purchase your companion eBook.

Apress®
THE EXPERT'S VOICE™